The Freedom Voyage - 75 Movements

The Road to Independence, from chains to change

Dr. Mili

INDIA · SINGAPORE · MALAYSIA

Copyright © Dr. Mili 2025
All Rights Reserved.

ISBN 979-8-89699-821-1

This book has been published with all efforts taken to make the material error-free after the consent of the author. However, the author and the publisher do not assume and hereby disclaim any liability to any party for any loss, damage, or disruption caused by errors or omissions, whether such errors or omissions result from negligence, accident, or any other cause.

While every effort has been made to avoid any mistake or omission, this publication is being sold on the condition and understanding that neither the author nor the publishers or printers would be liable in any manner to any person by reason of any mistake or omission in this publication or for any action taken or omitted to be taken or advice rendered or accepted on the basis of this work. For any defect in printing or binding the publishers will be liable only to replace the defective copy by another copy of this work then available.

Preface

India's struggle for freedom is not just a story of battles and politics—it is a story of dreams, sacrifices, and the will of countless people who believed in a better future. It is a journey that spans centuries, with moments of quiet resistance, fierce uprisings, and powerful ideas that challenged an empire. This book aims to tell the brief, not just through the well-known leaders, but through the many movements and individuals whose efforts often remain forgotten and many are unknown too.

From the first seeds of rebellion against foreign rule to the final victory in 1947, India's freedom was shaped by different kinds of struggles—some peaceful, some violent, some led by a few, and others by the masses. What unites them all is the idea that no people should live under oppression, and that freedom is worth fighting for, no matter the cost. These movements, while not as famous as the larger, mainstream movements like the Salt March or the Non-Cooperation Movement, played a crucial role in India's fight for independence. Each of these movements had its own cultural, social, and political context, and they demonstrate the broad and multi-faceted. Therefore, in writing this book, I have tried to capture the diversity of these movements—whether they were led by farmers in distant villages or revolutionaries in urban centers, by women fighting for their rights or students demanding change.

This book is not just a record of history; it is a reminder that freedom is never easy, and it is never won in one moment. It is something that is built over time, through the struggles, the dreams, and the determination of people. As you read these chapters, I hope you will see the power of ordinary individuals, the depth of their courage, and the unbreakable spirit that continues to inspire us all today.

I would like to thank Notion Press for publishing my book!

Author's Journey

Dr Mili is a dynamic new voice in the literary world, blending her deep passion for Indian culture and heritage with her academic background. Holding a Doctorate in Humanities with a focus on Social Service & Community Development, along with a Masters in Business Management, and Bachelors in Education and Commerce, Dr Mili has transformed her lifelong fascination with India's rich traditions into captivating books. When she's not lost in dusty cultural literature or documenting historical events and festivals, she's busy organizing cultural events.

In 2024, Dr Mili was honored with the *"Global Indian Cultural Icon Award"* by Indian Police Mitra Bharat & Dr. DS Rathod & Marshal Yoga Academy, and in 2022, she received the *"Outstanding Women Award"* for raising awareness of Indian culture abroad from *Women Icon powered by Times Women*.

Originally from Delhi, India, Dr Mili firmly believes that culture is essential to the growth of society and nations. Her interests include socializing, traveling, and connecting with people from various backgrounds. She fulfills her passion for culture by organizing events for children and celebrating Indian festivals, helping younger generations connect with the values, traditions, and rich heritage of India.

Dr Mili is currently serving as the President of the Indian Cultural Association of the Philippines (ICAP). She has been on the Board of ICAP since 2020. Before she moved to the Philippines in 2014, she was associated with an international school in Vietnam as a mathematics teacher for grades 11 and 12. Prior to that, she was associated with one of the largest Telecom operators as an HR manager based in Delhi, India. Her heart lies in uniting communities through events that showcase the diverse and vibrant cultures that define us.

This book would not have been completed without the support of her daughter Niharika Dhingra, her husband Ajay Dhingra, her mom Savita Mehta, her aunt Achla Bhandari, her MIL Saroj Dhingra and her friends.

Eighty percent of the profit from the sales will be dedicated to promoting and spreading Indian culture across the globe.

Table of Contents

Chapter 1:

Battle of Plassey (1757)

The Battle of Plassey was fought between the Nawab Of Bengal, Siraj-ud-daulah, and the British East India Company(Mir Jafar, Rai Durlabh, Jagat Seth) in the year 1757. The battle took place at the banks of the Bhagirathi river near Calcutta city and after the attack and plunder of Calcutta by Siraj-ud-daulah and the Black Hole of Calcutta tragedy. The Battle of Plassey is seen as the beginning of British colonial rule in India.

Majorly, the reasons for the Battle of Plassey to take place were:

- The rampant misuse of the trade privileges given to the British by the Nawab of Bengal

- Non-payment of tax and duty by the workers of the British East India Company

Other reasons that supported the coming of this battle were:

- Fortification of Calcutta by the British without the Nawab's permission

- Misleading Nawab on various fronts by British

- An asylum was provided to Nawab's enemy Krishna Das

The Battle of Plassey was a turning point in the history of British colonialism in India. After their victory, the British East India Company slowly gained more and more power in the region, eventually leading to full-blown colonisation. For Indian citizens, it is important to understand this moment in history and its lasting impact on our country.

THE BATTLE OF PLASSEY

Chapter 2:

Regulating Act of (1773)

The Regulating Act of 1773 was passed by the British Parliament to control the territories of the East India Company majorly in Bengal. It was the first parliamentary ratification and authorization defining the powers and authority of the East India Company concerning its Indian possessions.

This Act was passed in response to the company's mismanagement and financial crisis, to implement governance and accountability reforms. The Regulating Act of 1773 introduced changes in the structure of the Company's administration and marked the beginning of formal British Colonial rule in India. The act provided for the appointment of a Governor-General along with four Councillors in the Presidency of Fort William (Calcutta), jointly called the Governor-General in Council. The Governors in Councils at Madras and Bombay were brought under the control of Bengal, especially in matters of foreign policy. Now, they could not wage war against Indian states without Bengal's approval. The Regulating Act of 1773 laid the foundation of the Central Administration and Parliamentary Control.

THE REGULATING ACT OF 1773

The Regulating Act of 1773 established parliamentary control and centralized administration over the East India Company's territories in Bengal due to misgovernment and bankruptcy.

Chapter 3:

Pitt's India Act (1784)

The Pitt's India Act of 1784, also known as the **East India Company Act of 1784**, was a British Parliament act that established a dual system of control over India. The act's purpose was to address the shortcomings of the Regulating Act of 1773 and bring the East India Company's rule in India under closer control of the British government. Named after British Prime Minister **William Pitt** the Younger, this act marked a watershed moment in British Indian governance, laying the groundwork for the eventual establishment of the British Raj.

The Pitt's India Act introduced several key provisions to reform the governance of British India:

- The Board of Control took care of civil and military affairs. It comprised of 6 people:

- Secretary of State (Board President)

- Chancellor of the Exchequer

- Four Privy Councillors

- In this dual system of control, the company was represented by the Court of Directors and the British government by the Board of Control.

- The act mandated that all civil and military officers disclose their property in India and Britain within two months of their joining.

- The Governor-General's council's strength was reduced to three members. One of the three would be the Commander-in-Chief of the British Crown's army in India.

- The Presidencies of Madras and Bombay became subordinate to the Bengal Presidency. In effect, Calcutta became the capital of the British possessions in India.

Pitt's India Act established the system of dual control of India and these changes continued through 1858. The company's territories In India were called the "British possession in India" for the first time. The British Government was given complete control over the Company's affairs and its administration in India

PITT'S INDIA ACT OF 1784

Chapter 4:

Charter Acts, (1813) and (1833)

The Charter Act of 1813 passed by the British Parliament renewed the East India Company's charter for another 20 years. This is also called the East India Company Act, of 1813. The key provisions of the Charter Act of 1813 were, the end of the Company's monopoly over trading activities, the Company's dividend was 10.5 percent, one lakh rupees was assigned for the advancement of India's education system, the Board of Control was given more powers, and missionaries were allowed to spread religion in India. This act is important as it defined for the first time the constitutional position of British Indian territories. Due to the enactment of the Charter Acts of 1813 and 1833, the monopoly of the trade of the company with India was abolished except for the trade of tea. The Charter Act of 1833 was passed in the British Parliament which renewed the East India Company's charter for another 20 years. This was also called the Government of India Act 1833 or the Saint Helena Act 1833.

The Charter Act of 1833 was one among a series of Acts laid down by the British government to expand its administration in India. The regulations laid down by the Act had an influence on the political system of pre- independent India. Gradually, with the Charter Act 1833 implementation the British crown rule started gaining its control over Indian administration through the East India Company. Due to the enactment of the Charter Acts of 1813 and 1833, the monopoly of trade of the company with India was abolished except for the trade of tea.

CHARTER ACTS, 1813 AND 1833

The Charter Acts of 1813 and 1833 shaped British India's constitutional position, ending the East India Company's trade monopoly except for tea. These acts marked significant milestones in India's history.

Chapter 5:

The Paika Rebellion (1817) – Odisha

The Paika Rebellion is often considered the first war of independence against British rule in India, predating the 1857 revolt by four decades. The Paika Bidroha (Paika Rebellion) of 1817 took place nearly 40 years before the first sepoy mutiny.

It was led by the Paikas, the traditional militia of Odisha, against the British East India Company's oppressive policies. The Paikas (pronounced "paiko", literally 'foot soldiers'), were a class of military retainers had been recruited since the 16th century by kings in Odisha from a variety of social groups to render martial services in return for hereditary rent-free land (nish-kar jagirs) and titles.

The rebellion was sparked by the British-imposed land revenue system, and it was marked by large-scale guerrilla warfare. Although it was suppressed, it played an important role in the region's resistance to British colonialism.

On 24th December 2018, Prime Minister Narendra Modi released a commemorative stamp and coin on the Paika Rebellion. Along with the stamp and coin, PM announced to set up a Chair on Paika Rebellion in Bhubaneshwar's Utkal University. The Union Budget speech of 2017-18 mentioned the commemoration of the 200 years of the Paika Rebellion.

Paika Rebellion

Chapter 6:

Wahhabi Movement (1820s–1870s)

The aim of the Wahhabi movement was to overthrow the sikhs in Punjab and by extension the British all over India and restore the lost glory of the Muslim rulers of the subcontinent.

When the revolt of 1857 happened, the Wahhabi movement turned into an armed struggle against the British, prompting them to carry out extensive military operations against the followers of the movement. By 1870, the movement was completely suppressed. A pan-Islamic revivalist movement that also aimed to overthrow British rule, led by Syed Ahmed Barelvi.

Chapter 7:

Young Bengal Movement (1826)

The Young Bengal Movement was started by Henry Louis Vivian Derozio, who had come to Calcutta in 1826 and was appointed to the Hindu College as a teacher of English literature and History. The Young Bengal was a group of Bengali free thinkers. Derozio spread radical views through his teaching and the organization of a debate and discussion group on literature, history, philosophy, and science. Derozio literally enchanted the young students of Kolkata and carried about an intellectual movement amongst them through these efforts. They were inspired and excited by the spirit of free thought and revolt against the existing social and religious structure of Hindu society. The main aim of the Young Bengal Movement was to promote radical ideas through teachings and by organizing debates and discussions on Literature, History, Philosophy, and Science.

YOUNG BENGAL MOVEMENT (1826)

The Young Bengal Movement was started by Henry Louis Vivian Derozio, who had come to Calcutta in 1826 and was appointed to the Hindu College as a teacher of English literature and History.

Chapter 8:

Brahmo Samaj (1828)

Brahmo Samaj was a monotheistic section of Hinduism founded by Raja Ram Mohan Roy in 1828. The movement began through meetings of Bengalis in Calcutta in 1828. Debendranath Tagore, the father of Rabindranath Tagore, was a key member of the Brahmo Sabha. Brahmo Samaj Movement is one of the significant reform movements in India that aims to bring a renaissance to Bengal by fighting against the prevailing evil practices in the society, particularly the practice of Sati and the caste system, and emphasizing the educational, religious, and social reform. It was the first intellectual movement to eradicate bad practices of society successfully. Brahmo Samaj believed in the brotherhood of mankind and the fatherhood of God. It preached to stop animal sacrifice and offerings and love human beings.

The Brahmo Samaj played a significant role in the social, cultural, and political spheres of India, contributing indirectly to the Indian independence movement, its efforts in social reform and promoting progressive thinking played a crucial role in shaping the intellectual and social landscape of India, paving the way for future political movements that led to India's independence.

Brahmo Samaj: A progressive movement founded by Raja Ram Mohan Roy in 1828, fighting against social evils like Sati and caste system. Emphasized education, religious reform, and brotherhood of mankind.

Chapter 9:

Press Act, (1835)

Press Act of 1835 or Metcalfe Act, Metcalfe (governor general-1835-36) repealed the obnoxious 1823 ordinance and earned the epithet, "liberator of the Indian press". Newspapers played a significant role in the fight for Indian independence. The British government viewed the development and expansion of Indian newspapers as a threat, and as a result, it attempted several steps to stifle them using various acts and regulations. The Act positively impacted the growth of the press as many newspapers started publishing till stiff regulations were again imposed in 1857 due to the Revolt. The new Press Act (1835) required a printer/publisher to give a precise account of the premises of a publication and cease functioning. The press became the voice of leaders, a medium of information sharing, and a tool for criticism of the incumbent government and its policies.

The Development of the Indian Press can be largely traced in Three Distinct Phases:

- **Pre-1857 War of Independence** : Censorship of the Press Act (1799) , Licensing Regulations (1823), Metcalfe's Press Act (1835)

- **1857-1914**, Till the beginning of the First World War : Licensing Act of 1857, Vernacular Press Act 1878, The Indian Newspaper (Incitement to Offence) Act (1908), The Indian Press Act (1910)

- **1914-1947**, Till the enactment of the Indian Independence Act, 1947 : Defence of India Act (1915), The India Press (Emergency) Act (1931)

In conclusion, while the Press Act of 1835 was designed to curb dissent and control the spread of anti-British sentiments, it inadvertently played a role in uniting Indians against colonial oppression. The restriction on the press led to the emergence of a vibrant nationalist movement, contributing significantly to the eventual independence of India.

PRESS ACT OF 1835 OR METCALFE ACT

Press Act of 1835 or Metcalfe Act, the 'liberator of Indian press.' Repealing the oppressive 1823 ordinance, it empowered printers/publishers to voice opinions, share information, and critique the government. Press became a powerful tool for change.

Chapter 10:

Doctrine of Lapse (1848)

The Doctrine of Lapse was an annexation policy followed widely by Lord Dalhousie when he was India's Governor-General from 1848 to 1856. It was a strategy that was broadly utilised in India by the East India Company. The idea announced that each royal state under the organisation's vassalage would have its territory gained, assuming its ruler neglected to deliver a beneficiary. It was used as an administrative policy for the extension of British Paramountcy. Many Indian states lost their sovereignty and became British territories. This led to a lot of unrest among the Indian princes. A lot of people were unhappy with the 'illegal' nature of this doctrine and this was one of the causes of the Indian Revolt of 1857. Nana Sahib and the Rani of Jhansi had grievances against the British because the former's pension was stopped by the British after his foster father died, and the Rani's adopted son was denied the throne under the doctrine of lapse. Dalhousie returned to Britain in 1856.

Through Doctrine of Lapse many Kingdoms were annexed which are given below:

- The Kingdom of Satara was the 1st kingdom to be annexed through the Doctrine of Lapse in 1848.

- The Kingdom of Sambalpur was annexed in 1850.

- The Kingdom of Udaipur was annexed by Dalhousie through the Doctrine of Lapse in 1852.

- The Kingdom of Nagpur was annexed in 1853.

- The Kingdom of Jhansi was annexed in 1854.

- The final annexation through the Doctrine of Lapse was the Kingdom of Awadh in 1856.

The Doctrine of Lapse was ended by Lord Canning in 1859. After the Indian Revolt broke out in 1857, his governance was widely criticized as one of the causes of the rebellion.

DOCTRINE OF LAPSE (1848)

The Doctrine of Lapse was an annexation policy followed widely by Lord Dalhousie when he was India's Governor-General from 1848 to 1856. It was used as an administrative policy for the extension of British Paramountcy.

Chapter 11:

The Registration Act (1857)

Following the 1857 rebellion, the government imposed restrictions on the Indian press. The government reserved the right to grant and revoke licenses. The government was given the authority to prohibit the publication of any newspaper or book. This Act imposed licensing restrictions in addition to the Metcalfe Act's existing registration procedure. The government reserved the right to prohibit the publication and distribution of any book, newspaper, or printed matter. The Licensing Act of 1857 set a precedent for future press regulations in India. While it was repealed in 1865, its legacy persisted in subsequent press acts such as the Vernacular Press Act of 1878 and the Indian Press Act of 1910. These acts continued to impose restrictions on the press and were aimed at curbing nationalist sentiments. The repression of the press under the Licensing Act influenced the development of a more robust and resilient Indian press in the later years, which increasingly became a vehicle for promoting the nationalist agenda. As a result, the experience of dealing with such repressive laws shaped the advocacy for press freedom in independent India.

THE REGISTRATION ACT, 1857

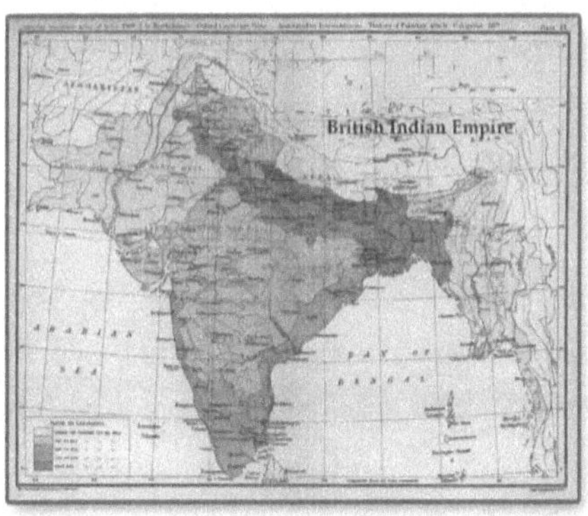

The Registration Act of 1857 in British India established a system to register documents like deeds, wills, and mortgages. It provided legal recognition, preventing fraud and settling property disputes by maintaining an official record and ensuring clear ownership rights.

Chapter 12:

The Mirzapur Uprising (1857) – Uttar Pradesh

The Mirzapur Uprising, during the First War of Indian Independence (1857), was a significant yet less-known revolt in the eastern part of Uttar Pradesh. The rebellion in Mirzapur was part of the larger mutiny against the British East India Company's forces. During the uprising of 1857, the district of Mirzapur also rose in rebellion against British rule. Leaders of Rajput clans like Adwant Singh and Jhurai Singh led this revolt. In June of 1857, Adwant Singh crowned himself the raja and started levying taxes. The uprising was led by local zamindars, peasantry, and soldiers who protested against the annexation of Indian states and the imposition of colonial rule. The local leadership, including **Rani of Jhansi** and **Kunwar Singh** of Bihar, had significant influence in motivating regional support for this uprising. The 1857 uprising, including events like those in Mirzapur, played a pivotal role in fostering Indian nationalism. Even though the immediate result was the defeat of the rebels, it marked the beginning of a collective national consciousness and laid the foundation for future struggles for independence. It made clear the Indian desire to break free from British control, signaling that the demand for self-rule would not be easily suppressed.

The Mirzapur Uprising of 1857, though not as prominent as other parts of the rebellion, was a vital part of the First War of Indian Independence. It contributed to the growing resistance against British rule, showed the unity of different groups in opposing colonial power, and was part of the larger momentum that eventually led to India's independence in 1947. While it was not successful in its immediate goals, the uprising and the larger 1857 rebellion inspired future generations of Indians to continue the struggle for freedom.

THE UPRISING OF 1857

Chapter 13:

Government of India Act, (1858)

The Government of India Act 1858 was an Act of the British parliament that transferred the government and territories of the East India Company to the British Crown. It created the position of Secretary of State for India, with the additional position of a British Cabinet Minister in charge of Indian affairs and made him directly responsible to the British Parliament. Established the India Office in London to assist and support the Secretary of State and rationalized the administration and policy implementation with respect to Indian governance.

The company's rule over British territories in India came to an end and it was passed directly to the British government. This act abolished the dual government of Pitt's India Act. This act also ended the doctrine of lapse. The Act provided for the foundation of the Indian Civil Services, which were tasked with administering the country. Indians were also permitted to join the military.

There were many Indirect Contributions to Indian Independence like increased Resentment and Nationalist Sentiment, Rise of Indian Political Awareness was a key factor in the eventual push for self-governance and independence, Foundation for Future Rebellions and Movements

The Government of India Act of 1858 did not directly contribute to India's independence, as it strengthened British control over the subcontinent. However, its imposition led to increased political consciousness and nationalist fervor in India. By consolidating British power, it sparked greater resentment and the desire for self-rule, which would eventually culminate in the Indian independence movement and the eventual freedom of India in 1947.

GOVERNMENT OF INDIA ACT, 1858

The Government of India Act 1858 was an Act of the British parliament
that transferred the government and territories of the East India
Company to the British Crown.

Chapter 14:

Jaintia and Garo Rebellion (1860–1870s)

The Jaintia and Garo Rebellion, which took place in the 1860s and 1870s, was a significant resistance movement in the North-Eastern part of India, specifically in present-day Meghalaya. The rebellion was sparked by the British construction of a strategic road connecting the Brahmaputra Valley with Sylhet. The Jaintias and Garos, recognizing the road's importance for the movement of British troops, opposed its construction. The unrest began in 1827 when the Jaintias attempted to halt the work, and it soon spread to the Garo hills. In response, the British burned several villages belonging to the Jaintias and Garos. Tensions further escalated when the British introduced House Tax and Income Tax in the 1860s, which added to the grievances of the local population. The British authorities took decisive actions against the rebellion. The Jaintias' leader, U Kiang Nongbah, was captured and publicly hanged, while the Garo leader, Pa Togan Sangma, was defeated by the British forces. Although the Jaintia and Garo Rebellion was ultimately quelled by the British, it represented a significant resistance against British colonial rule in the region. The rebellion highlighted the discontent and resistance of the local communities against British policies and encroachments on their land and resources. The memory of the rebellion and the sacrifices made by its leaders continue to shape the collective identity and historical consciousness of the people in Meghalaya

Chapter 15:

The Aligarh Movement (1863)

The Aligarh movement started in 1875 to establish a modern education system for the Muslim population of British India. The movement's name derives from the fact that its core and origins lay in the city of Aligarh in Northern India along with the founding of the Muhammadan Anglo-Oriental College. The Aligarh Movement has made a lasting contribution to the political emancipation of Indian Muslims. It influenced several other contemporary movements to a great extent that it caused the emergence of other socio-religious movements during the 19th century. There was hostility between the Muslim community and the British due to its participation in the revolt of 1857. Hence, it stayed away from English education. To address this issue, Sir Syed Ahmad Khan started a new movement known as the Aligarh Reformation Movement. In 1863, he established the Mohammadan Liberty Society to debate and discuss religious, political and social issues of society.

The Aligarh Movement (1863) was instrumental in educating and modernizing the Muslim community in India. This movement was primarily focused on the educational upliftment of Muslims, but its broader influence had significant implications for India's fight for independence. While it did not directly fight for independence, its emphasis on modern education, social reform, and intellectual growth played a crucial role in shaping the future leaders of the Indian independence struggle. The movement fostered a spirit of political awareness and unity, contributing to the broader nationalist cause and paving the way for the eventual independence of India in 1947.

Standing R to L : chaubdar, Syed Zain uddin, Maulana Shibli,
                  Mustafa Khan of Khurja, Syed Ahmad Ali, Nawab Nazir Jang, peon
Sitting   : Maulvi Iqbal Ali (judge), Zain ul Abidin, Qazi Raza Hasan (Patna),
                  Sir Syed, Mohsin ul Mulk, Syed Imtiaz Ali.
Ground   : son of Nawab Nazir Jang

Chapter 16:

Deoband Movement (1866)

The Deoband Movement emerged in the aftermath of the Revolt of 1857, which marked the formal establishment of British rule in India. The movement's founders, including Maulana Muhammad Qasim Nanautavi and Maulana Rashid Ahmad Gangohi, were deeply concerned about the decline of Islamic traditions and the growing influence of Western culture and education. Mahmud Deobandi was the first teacher, while Mahmud Hasan Deobandi was the first student. Deoband's influence as a school and a transitional socio-religious movement stemmed first from its new style of Islamic education, which included an appointed faculty, a fixed curriculum, and regular examinations. This structure, as well as the methods used to raise funds, were inspired by the English educational model and the organization of voluntary associations. Through their students and the numerous fatwas on issues of proper religious practice, the Deobandis gained widespread respect and influence in the North and beyond.

The Deobandis have been outspoken opponents of Sufi devotional practices. This Socio-Religious Reform Movement spread among Muslims the clear teachings of the Quran and the Hadis. It opposed the thoughts propagated by the Aligarh Movement.It was aimed at the moral and religious regeneration of the Muslim community. The formation of the Indian National Congress was welcomed by it.

It had an indirect Contribution to Indian Independence like it indirectly influenced the growth of Muslim political activism in India, its leaders inspired the formation of various political groups, including the Jamaat-e-Islami and the All India Muslim League. These groups played significant roles in Indian politics, including the demand for an independent India. The Deoband leaders' refusal to adopt Western cultural norms and their insistence on the preservation of Indian identity helped foster a sense of cultural pride and resistance to the British. This cultural and intellectual resistance to colonialism was a key part of the larger Indian nationalist movement. The Deoband school of thought promoted the idea that the Indian Muslim community should unite with other Indian communities to fight for independence.

While the Deoband Movement of 1866 was initially focused on religious and educational reforms within the Muslim community, it played an important indirect role in the Indian independence movement. By fostering anti-British sentiment, promoting cultural resistance, and contributing to the rise of Muslim political activism, the Deoband Movement helped lay the intellectual and ideological foundation for the Indian struggle for independence. Its influence extended beyond religious education, making it an integral part of India's fight against colonial rule.

Deoband Ulema's
Movement for the
Freedom of India

Chapter 17:

Prarthana Samaj (1867)

The Prarthana Samaj, a leading society for socio-religious reform was established on 31 March 1867 in Bombay by Atmaram Panduranga and went on to wield a good deal of influence in western India and to a lesser extent in southern India.Prarthana samaj is also known as a 'prayer society' in Sanskrit. It was based on earlier reform movements and spread to Southern India by Telugu reformer Kundukuri Veersalingam.

Prarthana Samaj was built on several core principles aimed at reforming society and religion by encouraging rationalism, social justice, and spiritual development. The key principles of Prarthana Samaj include: Rational Approach to Religion, Social Equality, Religious Reform,

Education for All, Opposition to Superstitions and Universal Brotherhood.

Prarthana Samaj Four Point Social Agenda

- Criticism of the caste system

- Female education

- Remarriage of Widows

- Increasing the marriage age for both men and women

The movement's commitment to social justice and equality fostered a sense of nationalism, encouraging many to participate in the struggle for independence. The ideas propagated by Prarthana Samaj found expression in various social and political movements across India.

By advocating for women's rights, the Samaj contributed to the larger movement for women's empowerment, which later became an important part of the independence struggle. Empowered women became active participants in political and social movements, including the independence movement, where leaders like Sarojini Naidu and Kamini

Roy emerged as prominent figures. The reformers of the Prarthana Samaj, like M.G. Ranade, were closely associated with the Indian National Congress (INC). Their participation in political processes and support for democratic reforms provided ideological support for the INC's objectives of self-rule and national unity. This connection reinforced the alignment between social reforms and the larger goals of the Indian independence movement.

The Prarthana Samaj (1867), though primarily a social and religious reform movement, contributed significantly to the Indian independence struggle. By advocating for social justice, rational education, religious tolerance, and unity, it laid the groundwork for the intellectual and political awakening that would fuel the independence movement. The reforms promoted by the Samaj not only advanced social change but also helped shape the nationalist movement, fostering unity and a collective desire for political self-determination, ultimately leading to India's independence.

PRARTHANA SAMAJ 1867

The Prarthana Samaj, a leading society for socio-religious reform was established on 31 March 1867 in Bombay by Atmaram Panduranga and went on to wield a good deal of influence in western India and to a lesser extent in southern India.

Chapter 18:

Indian Council Act (1892)

The Indian Councils Act, also known as the Morley-Minto Reforms, increased the number of elected Indian representatives in the legislative councils. The Indian Council Act of 1892 was introduced by the British parliament to amend the existing constitutional provisions in the country. The principle of representation was initiated through this act. The district boards, universities, municipalities, chambers of commerce and zamindars were authorised to recommend members to the provincial councils. The legislative councils were empowered to make new laws and repeal old laws with the permission of the Governor-General.

The demands made by the Indian National Congress in session were:

- A test of ICS was conducted in England and India simultaneously

- Legislative council reforms such as election in place of nomination adoption

- Annexation of Upper Burma was opposed

- Reduction of military expenditure

- Chats about forbidden financials should be granted

The reforms made during the Indian Council Act 1892 were also known by the name "Morley–Minto Reforms" as they had contributions from both lord Minto and John Morley. They were behind passing the Act in the parliament in the year 1909 under the name Indian Councils Act.

The Indian Councils Act of 1892 was an important milestone in the constitutional history of British India, as it marked a step toward the inclusion of Indians in the legislative process. Though it did not grant full political rights or self-rule, the Act played a key role in the development of political awareness and the push for greater representation, ultimately contributing to India's independence movement.

It played a pivotal role in Indian Independence. The Indian Councils Act of 1892 contributed to the political awakening of Indians. Although the reforms were modest, the Act increased the political ambitions of Indians. The limited inclusion of Indians in the councils highlighted the need for more extensive reforms, which were eventually demanded by political organizations such as the Indian National Congress (INC). The Act provided a platform for moderate leaders like Dadabhai Naoroji, Gopal Krishna Gokhale, and Bal Gangadhar Tilak to voice their concerns and push for greater self-governance. The increased participation in councils allowed Indian leaders to develop a national political identity and begin working towards a united goal of self-rule. While the British maintained control, the Act contributed to the formation of a more organized political opposition and encouraged the growth of the Indian National Congress as a key political player, laying the groundwork for future demands for self-rule and independence.

The Indian Councils Act of 1892 was a modest but significant step toward political reform in British India. While it did not provide Indians with substantial power, it increased political representation, fostered political awareness, and ignited demands for further reforms. It laid the groundwork for future political movements and contributed to the growing sense of nationalism and unity among Indians, which ultimately played a crucial role in the Indian independence movement. The Act also highlighted the limitations of British colonial rule, fueling the desire for self-governance and, eventually, independence.

THE INDIAN COUNCIL ACT, 1892

Also known as the Morley-Minto Reforms, increased the number of elected Indian representatives in the legislative councils. It also introduced separate electorates, which reinforced communal divisions between Hindus and Muslims.

Chapter 19:

Ramakrishna Movement (1897)

Ramakrishna Movement was initiated by Swami Vivekananda to spread the universal message of Vedanta in the light of Sri Ramakrishna and to work for the alleviating of the poor and the downtrodden with the motto 'for one's liberation and the good of the world'.

The Ramakrishna Mission was formed in May 1897 with aims purely spiritual and humanitarian.

- Ramakrishna Math and Ramakrishna Mission are twin organizations that form the core of a worldwide spiritual movement known as the Ramakrishna Movement or Vedanta Movement.

- The Ramakrishna Mission is a philanthropic, volunteer organization founded by Sri Ramakrishna's chief disciple Swami Vivekananda on May 1, 1897.

- The Mission conducts extensive work in health care, disaster relief, rural management, tribal welfare, elementary and higher education, and culture.

- It uses the combined efforts of hundreds of ordered monks and thousands of householder disciples.

- The Mission bases its work on the principles of karma yoga.

The Ramakrishna Movement contributed a lot to Indian Independence. Vivekananda's teachings instilled a sense of pride in Indian culture and spirituality. This was especially important during a time when British colonial rule sought to undermine India's traditions. Swami Vivekananda's call for national revival and self-reliance deeply resonated with the Indian elite and the youth. His message that India needed to revitalize its spiritual and intellectual life laid the groundwork for the emergence of Indian nationalism. The ideas he promoted influenced many leaders of the independence struggle, including Subhas Chandra

Bose, Lala Lajpat Rai, and Bal Gangadhar Tilak, who sought to make India a united, self-reliant, and independent nation. Vivekananda's ideas helped bridge divides within Indian society, advocating for unity among the Hindu community while emphasizing the importance of social reforms. This vision of unity later became a significant aspect of the Indian National Congress (INC) and its struggle for independence. His emphasis on self-reliance and self-improvement paralleled the growing Swadeshi Movement.

The Ramakrishna Movement (1897), spearheaded by Swami Vivekananda, played an influential role in the intellectual and cultural revival of India during the colonial period. Through his teachings of spiritual empowerment, social reform, and national unity, Vivekananda helped ignite a sense of Indian pride and self-respect that was essential in the fight for independence. His efforts to encourage self-reliance, self-improvement, and unity inspired a generation of leaders and activists who contributed significantly to the struggle for India's freedom. The Ramakrishna Movement was not only a spiritual awakening but also an important catalyst for the nationalist movement that led to India's eventual independence.

Chapter 20:

Partition of Bengal (1905)

The partition of Bengal took place in 1905 as a result of British India's desire for greater administrative efficiency. This move, orchestrated by Lord Curzon, the Viceroy of India, aimed to create two more manageable provinces – East Bengal and Assam, and West Bengal.

The main causes of Partition of Bengal 1905 proposed by Lord Curzon were widespread political unrest and opposition across the region, Bengalis strongly opposed the partition, viewing it as an attack on their national identity and calling for the reunification of Bengal, the Indian National Congress criticized the partition, citing racial considerations and condemning the British government's strategy. The British "divide and rule" strategy was perceived to underlie the partition, aimed at undermining nationalist sentiments within India. Opposition to the partition led to the rise of nationalist movements such as the Swadeshi and Boycott movements, advocating for economic self-reliance and boycotts of British goods. The religious divisions caused by the partition also contributed to the formation of the Muslim League in 1906, further shaping the political landscape of India. All fragments of the Indian society were integrated on a single platform for the first time against colonial rule, thereby laying the grounds for further movements.

PARTITION OF BENGAL (1905)

The Partition of Bengal (1905) by the British Raj authorities sparked the Swadeshi and Boycott movements, leading to significant protests. Later annulled in 1911 due to widespread unrest.

Chapter 21:

The Swadeshi Movement (1905–1908)

The Swadeshi movement was a self-sufficiency movement that was a part of the Indian independence movement and helped to shape Indian nationalism. The Swadeshi movement began in 1905 as a unified reaction to Bengal's partition and lasted until 1908. It was the most successful of the pre-Gandhian movements. After the British Government's decision to partition Bengal was made public in December 1903, there was widespread dissatisfaction among Indians. In response, the Swadeshi movement was formally launched on August 7, 1905, from Town Hall Calcutta, with the goal of reducing reliance on foreign goods in favor of domestic production.

The Swadeshi movement was quite different from previous movements led by national leaders. This movement pursued a programme of direct political action in opposition to the policy of 'prayer and petition.' During its early stages, the Swadeshi movement attempted to have Bengal's partition annulled. The 'boycott' aspect of the Swadeshi movement aimed at economically pressuring Manchester mill-owners so that they could put pressure on the British government to annul Partition. The Swadeshi movement's cultural significance was also significant. During the Swadeshi period, Bengali literature flourished. Rabindranath Tagore and Rajanikanto Sen's patriotic compositions and creations magically touched the patriotic sense of the masses.

Overall, the Swadeshi movement remains an important chapter in India's struggle for independence, highlighting the challenges and complexities involved in challenging colonial rule and promoting nationalistic aspirations. It served as a precursor to later movements and laid the foundation for the larger fight against British imperialism in the years to come.

THE SWADESHI MOVEMENT (1905)

Chapter 22:

The Split in the Congress (1907)

The conflict between the various nationalist strands culminated in the Surat Split in December 1907. Rash Behari Ghosh presided over the Surat Congress session in 1907, despite opposition from Tilak and others. At the Surat session, Congress leaders were divided into two factions: Moderates and Extremists. The Surat Split of 1907 was a pivotal division within the Indian National Congress between the Moderates, who advocated for gradual reforms, and the Extremists, who demanded immediate and direct action against British rule.

The Surat Split was a watershed moment in the history of India's Nationalist Movement. It represented a shift in the government's policy and attitude toward nationalist moderates on the government side. The Surat Split was the direct cause of the Minto-Morley Reform of 1909. Both parties have been greatly weakened as a result of the split. The Surat Split of 1907 highlighted deep-seated ideological differences within the Indian National Congress and underscored the need for a united nationalist movement against British rule. The split weakened the Congress and allowed the British government to suppress the Extremists, ultimately stalling the momentum of the independence movement until new leaders and strategies emerged in the following decade.

THE SPLIT IN THE CONGRESS (1907)

Chapter 23:

Minto-Morley Constitutional Reforms (1909)

The Minto-Morley Reforms, also known as the Indian Councils Act of 1909, was a series of constitutional reforms introduced in India during British colonial rule. The Indian Councils Act 1909 was introduced by the British government in India as a step towards including Indians in government. It is also referred to as the Morley-Minto reforms named after the two British officials who played a key role in its drafting: Lord Minto and Lord John Morley, who were the Viceroy and Secretary of State of British India respectively in 1905-10.

The reforms aimed to increase Indian participation in the legislative process while still maintaining British control over governance. Key provisions of the Minto-Morley Reforms included:

- Introduction of separate electorates
- Expansion of legislative councils
- Introduction of the principle of communal representation
- Enhanced legislative powers

It played a significant role in the Indian independence movement by marking a shift in British policy toward India. These reforms were introduced by the British government to address the growing discontent among Indians and to manage the increasing demands for political participation. While the Minto-Morley Reforms did not directly lead to independence, they laid the foundation for future political developments and were part of the larger process that eventually resulted in India gaining independence in 1947.

MINTO-MORLEY CONSTITUTIONAL REFORMS (1909)

The Minto-Morley Reforms, also known as the Indian Councils Act of 1909, was a series of constitutional reforms introduced in India during British colonial rule. They were named after the then Viceroy of India, Lord Minto, and the Secretary of State for India, John Morley.

Chapter 24:

Komagata Maru Incident (1914)

The Komagata Maru was a coal-transport Japanese steamship that had been converted into a passenger ship by Hong Kong-based businessman Gurdit Singh. It set off from Hong Kong in April 1914, reaching Vancouver's harbor a month later with 376 people on board, most of them Sikhs. A ship from Canada by the name of Komagata Maru that was carrying immigrants from India was sent back. Several of the ship's passengers were killed or detained in a clash with the British police as it headed back to India. The Komagata Maru episode attracted worldwide attention and condemnation for the violation of human rights and racism. The episode further inspired the Ghadar party to engage in its struggle against colonial rule, and therefore it indirectly gave a fillip to the Indian struggle for freedom.

Throughout the journey, the Komagata maru stopped at various ports where political lectures helped rally support from neighbouring countries. The Asian Exclusion Act only allowed politicians to doubt Whiteman's burden argument because they refused to accept that "burden."

The Ghadar Party used the tragedy to rally support for a massive revolt against the British Empire. As a result, the Komagata Maru incident may be seen as a watershed point in Indian political history. It infuriated the public and provided a forum for assaults on British citizens

KOMAGATAMARU INCIDENT. 1914

Chapter 25:

The Ghadar Movement (1914)

The Ghadar Party was an international political movement consisting of expatriate Indians to overthrow British rule in India. The official founding has been dated to a meeting on 15 July 1913 in Astoria, Oregon, the United States of America. The Ghadar Movement was a significant turning point in India's quest for independence. Early in the 20th century, several stringent immigration laws based on racial discrimination were put in place to reduce the number of Indian immigrants coming to Canada in search of employment.

- After the brutal British repression, the Ghadar Movement started to wane. 1917 saw the Ghadar Party split into a Communist and a Socialist faction following the end of World War I.

- The Ghadar movement might be characterized as a story of extraordinary bravery, labor, and toil that affected every Indian living in foreign countries.

- The arrests, the trial, the shooting, and deportations all attracted sensational publicity from the American press which heightened suspicion towards Asian Indians. In the 1920s, however, the Ghadar Party was reorganized and it continued as a focal point for Punjabi and Sikh identity until the time of Indian independence in 1947.

GADAR MOVEMENT
NRIs FIGHT FOR INDIA'S INDEPENDENCE

Chapter 26:

Lucknow Pact (1916)

The Lucknow Pact is an agreement between the Indian National Congress (INC) and the All India Muslim League (AIML) reached at a joint session of both parties held in Lucknow in 1916. The pact was important in that it enhanced the League's power in Indian politics and established communalism as an unavoidable part of Indian politics despite the apparent bonhomie between the two communities at the session. The ideological differences between the two organizations were sharp as the Muslim League's work was focused on community-specific demands, while the Congress claimed to represent India as a whole. The signing of the Lucknow pact was seen as an important development in the articulation of demands of the Indians and for being a message of communal unity and harmony among the people.

Reforms suggested in the Lucknow Pact

- Self-government in India.

- Abolition of the Indian Council.

- Separation of the executive from the judiciary.

- Salaries of the Secretary of State for Indian Affairs are to be paid from British coffers and not Indian funds.

- The number of Muslims in the provincial legislatures is to be laid down for each province.

- Separate electorates for all communities until a joint electorate is demanded by all.

- Introduction of a system of weightage for minority representation (it implied giving minorities more representation than their share in the population).

- Increasing the term of the Legislative Council to 5 years.

The Lucknow Pact marked a rare moment of political unity between the Congress, which largely represented Hindus, and the Muslim League, which represented Muslim interests. This cooperation strengthened the demand for self-rule from the British, showing a united front of major Indian communities seeking constitutional reforms. The success of the Lucknow Pact showed the British that Indian political parties could cooperate across communal lines, making it difficult for them to use "divide and rule" tactics effectively. This set the stage for increasing demands for self-rule and later contributed to the growing momentum for India's independence.

The Lucknow Pact was a landmark in the Indian independence movement, as it represented political unity, brought Muslims into the mainstream of the independence struggle, and laid the groundwork for future demands for full independence from British rule.

Chapter 27:

The Home Rule Movement (1916–1918)

The Indian Home Rule Movement (1916-1918) was founded in British India on the lines of the Irish Home Rule Movement. It aimed to attain home rule or self-government for India under the British Empire along the lines of countries like Canada and Australia. The Home Rule Movement served as the country's response to the First World War and a powerful means to express opposition to British rule. It was started by Bal Gangadhar Tilak at Belgaum in April 1916 and later by Annie Besant in Madras in September 1916.

This movement was targeted at achieving self-rule, without the interference of the British Government. The movement sought to demonstrate the strength of India and its people by raising political awareness and assembling a bigger political representation for the nation in opposition to British Rule. This movement resulted in the 1917 Montagu Declaration, which said that there would be a greater representation of Indians in the administration, fostering the growth of institutions for self-governance and finally bringing about responsible governments in India. The turning point in the movement was in 1917 when the Madras Government decided to place Annie Besant and her associates, B P Wadia and George Arundale, under arrest. The movement gained substantial support from educated Indians. It had approximately 40,000 members in 1917 after the two leagues combined. Their internment became the pivot for nationwide protests, and the popularity of the movement soared. The government had to back down and adopt a conciliatory approach.

The Home Rule Movement played a significant role in setting the stage for the national freedom movement under the leadership of Mahatma Gandhi.

HOME RULE MOVEMENT – 1916-18

Home Rule Movement served as the country's response to the First World War and a powerful means to express opposition to British rule. It was started by Bal Gangadhar Tilak at Belgaum in April 1916 and later by Annie Besant in Madras in September 1916.

Chapter 28:

Champaran Movement in Bihar (1917)

The Champaran Satyagraha of 1917 was the first Satyagraha movement led by Gandhi in India and is considered a historically important revolt in the Indian Independence Movement. It was a farmer's uprising that took place in Champaran district of Bihar, India, during the British colonial period. The farmers were protesting against having to grow indigo with barely any payment for it. When Gandhi returned to India from South Africa in 1915, and saw peasants in northern India oppressed by indigo planters, he tried to use the same methods that he had used in South Africa to organize mass uprisings by people to protest against injustice.

Champaran Satyagraha was the first popular satyagraha movement. The Champaran Satyagraha gave direction to India's youth and freedom struggle, which was between moderates who prescribed Indian participation within the British colonial system, and the extremists from Bengal who advocated the use of violent methods to topple the British colonialists in India. The peasants in Champaran had campaigned several times before for an end to the tinkathia system, but had not been successful. It was the peasants themselves who called in Gandhi for support, although they began to massively support him after he was arrested. This is one of Mahatma Gandhi's first exercises in nonviolent civil disobedience in India. Afterwards, Gandhi led a series of nonviolent civil disobedience campaigns around India. On August 15, 1947, the Indian Independence Act was passed—since then known as Indian Independence Day.

CHAMPARAN MOVEMENT IN BIHAR, 1917

Chapter 29:

Ahmedabad Satyagraha in Gujarat (1918)

Ahmedabad Satyagraha is also known as Ahmedabad Mill Strike was the first hunger strike led by Mahatma Gandhi. The Ahmedabad Satyagraha was led by Mahatma Gandhi in 1918 after he returned from South Africa just at the turn of the twentieth century. Ahmedabad has been witness to various landmark events from the Indian freedom movement, including Mahatma Gandhi's hunger strike in support of Ahmedabad Mill Workers.

After the Champaran Satyagraha movement in 1917, the Ahmedabad mill strike grew to become the largest civil disobedience movement of its time. During this strike, Gandhi first used two nonviolent strategies: a hunger strike and satyagraha. Ahmedabad belonged to the Bombay presidency when Britain was in power. During the British occupation, Ahmedabad's cotton industry prospered and the city became a significant commercial center. The employees and owners of a cotton mill in Ahmedabad engaged in a labor dispute in 1918. The mill's owners wanted to take away the employees' rightful plague bonus. In contrast, the mill owners were only willing to offer a 20% pay raise, despite the workers' demands for a 50% pay increase. Gandhi led a nonviolent strike and went on a hunger strike to defend the rights of the working class. Like other satyagrahas, the Ahmedabad mill satyagraha was successful. Gandhi first used the strategy of a hunger strike during the Ahmedabad mill strike, as was previously mentioned. The mill owners were stirred up by his fast, and they were forced to give in to the demands that were made.

Gandhi ji was introduced to the masses through these encounters, and he actively promoted their interests for the rest of his life. In actuality, he was the first nationalist leader of India to relate his life and way of life to that of the common people. He became known as the face of nationalist, rebellious, and poor India over time.

AHMEDABAD SATYAGRAHA IN GUJARAT, 1918

Chapter 30:

Kheda Satyagraha in Gujarat (1918)

The satyagraha movement in the Kheda district of Gujarat in India was led by Mahatma Gandhi, in which Gandhi agreed to help the peasant movement for income remission in Kheda at the request of local peasant leaders. The movement is known as Kheda Satyagraha or Kheda Andolan or Kheda Movement. During this period, the middle-class, modern-educated class became more involved in peasant resistance activities. It sowed the seeds of patriotism among the peasantry as well. Various leaders play a major role in the Kheda movement. The main leader of the whole movement is Mahatma Gandhi. Along with this, Sardar Vallabhbhai Patel played the role of the main follower of Mahatma Gandhi during this movement. Various lawyers from different corners of the world take part in this movement. These are:

- Shankarlal Banker

- Narhari Parikh

- Mahadev Desai

- Indulal Yagnik

- Narhari Parikh

- Ravi Shankar Vyas

- Mohanlal Pandya

After continuous efforts for several months, Mahatma Gandhi and his supporters, including peasants, were successful. The British government had accepted this agreement and unseized the lands of all peasants. However, Britishers also suspended the tax of 1919. Along with this, the British government also had to return those lands they had previously seized. Kheda Satyagraha is one of the big achievements of peasants in the history of India.

The achievement of Kheda Satyagraha is written among the greatest achievements of Indian history. The thing about this movement is that the reformers do not practice even a single violent activity during the entire movement. Although, they are put forward in a very decent and humble way. The hard struggle of Kheda Satyagraha has embarked a new light among the peasants of India, which resulted in the growth of Nationality among citizens. The success of Kheda Satyagraha has astonished the entire country and given hope of an independent India. The Indian citizens get motivated for their achievement of independence.

Chapter 31:

Rowlatt Satyagraha (1919)

Rowlatt Satyagraha was one of the first movements launched by Mahatma Gandhi, after his arrival in India. It began in 1919 in Mumbai City, Maharashtra, against the oppressive Anarchical and Revolutionary Crimes Act of 1919, popularly known as the Rowlatt Act. The Act was based on the recommendations of the Sedition Committee headed by Sir Sidney Rowlatt. It essentially sought to criminalize dissent, empowered the government to suppress political activities, and allowed the detention of political prisoners without trial or judicial review for two years.

The Rowlatt Satyagraha established Gandhi's leadership. His ability to cut across barriers of religion, class, caste and region and unite millions of Indians in a common cause was unparalleled. The nationalists realised that constitutional means alone would not persuade the British to relinquish power. The Rowlatt Strike shifted the struggle towards mass agitations and non-cooperation as viable strategies to put pressure on the colonial authorities. It paved the way for Gandhi's Non-Cooperation Movement in 1920.

Newspaper notices and handbills were printed and distributed in an effort to draw large crowds to the protest at Bombay Chowpatty on 06 April. This day later came to be known as the Black Day. The Rowlatt Satyagraha marked a shift in Indian nationalist politics from being the politics of 'a select few classes' to becoming the 'politics of the masses.'

ROWLATT SATYAGRAHA, 1919

Chapter 32:

Jallianwala Bagh Massacre (1919)

The Jallianwala Bagh Massacre, also known as the Massacre of Amritsar, was an incident that took place on April 13, 1919. That day, British troops fired on a large crowd of unarmed Indians in an open space called the Jallianwala Bagh in Amritsar. Several hundred people, including children, died, and hundreds more were wounded. This incident is a turning point in India's modern history that led to Gandhi's full commitment to the cause of Indian nationalism and independence from Britain.

This massacre exposed the inhuman approach of the British when the British troop cold-bloodedly opened fire on an unarmed crowd without any warning by General Dyer who had assembled at the enclosed park for the public meeting that was banned. There was no official data on the number of deaths during the Jallianwala Bagh Massacre. But the official enquiry of the British revealed that there were 379 deaths and the Congress quoted more than 1000 people died in the massacre.

In December 1919, the congress session was held at Amritsar. It was attended by a large number of people, including peasants. It was clear that the brutalities had only added fuel to the fire and made the people's determination stronger to fight for their freedom and against oppression.

JALLIANWALA BAGH MASSACRE, 1919

Jallianwala Bagh Massacre: The Jallianwala Bagh Massacre, also known as the Massacre of Amritsar, was an incident that took place on April 13, 1919. That day, British troops fired on a large crowd of unarmed Indians in an open space called the Jallianwala Bagh in Amritsar.

Chapter 33:

Diarchy (1919) and Montagu-Chelmsford Reforms or Government of India Act, (1919)

In 1918, Edwin Montagu, the Secretary of State, and Lord Chelmsford, the Viceroy, produced their scheme of constitutional reforms, known as the Montagu-Chelmsford (or Mont-Ford) Reforms, which led to the enactment of the Government of India Act of 1919. The diarchy was implemented in eight provinces:

- Assam, Bengal, Bihar and Orissa, Central Provinces, United Provinces, Bombay, Madras, and Punjab.

- The provincial governments were given more powers under the system of Dyarchy.

The Government of India Act 1919 was an act of the British Parliament that was introduced for an increase of participation for administration by the Indians for their country. From 1919 until 1929, this statute was in effect for ten years.Diarchy was applied on a state-by-state basis. Diarchy refers to the presence of two governments in which one is responsible and the other is not. The Montagu-Chelmsford Reforms of 1919 recommended granting voting rights to all women above the age of 21. The most important inclusion of the act was the "end of benevolent despotism" to introduce a responsible government in India. This act was in action for 10 years from 1919 to 1929.

At the national, provincial, and local branches of administration, the Act ushered in reforms. It formed a two-tiered government and contains two listings for all actions regulated by the government. The Government of India (GOI) act, 1919, signalled the administration's desire to gradually introduce responsible government in India being the first time for them. The people were granted more administrative power, and the government's administrative pressure was considerably lessened.

The Montagu-Chelmsford Reforms (1919) represented an attempt by the British to placate Indian demands for self-governance but were seen as inadequate by Indian leaders. While they did provide more Indian representation, they still maintained British control over key areas of governance. Diarchy introduced a system that limited Indian powers in provincial governance, leading to frustration and contributing to the broader independence movement. While these reforms represented a step toward acknowledging Indian participation in governance, they also acted as a catalyst for more determined efforts toward complete independence.

DIARCHY (1919) & MONTAGU-CHELMSFORD REFORMS OR GOVERNMENT OF INDIA ACT, 1919

Chapter 34:

Khilafat Movement (1919–24)

The Khilafat Movement was launched by Muhammad Ali and Shaukat Ali. The movement was aimed to unite the Muslim community under the umbrella of a unified national movement. At the Calcutta Session of the Congress in September 1920, Gandhiji convinced other leaders to start a Non-Cooperation Movement in support of Khilafat Movement. The Khilafat Movement (1919-1924), was a pan-Islamic, political protest campaign launched by Muslims in British India to influence the British Government and to protect the Ottoman empire during the aftermath of the First World War.

The Khilafat Movement holds significance in Indian history. It showcased the political consciousness and unity of Indian Muslims in their support for a cause beyond their immediate national interests. It also fostered Hindu-Muslim unity and cooperation. It promoted a sense of solidarity against British colonial rule. The movement had an alliance with the Indian National Congress under Mahatma Gandhi's leadership. This demonstrated the convergence of different religious and political groups in the struggle for independence.

The Khilafat Movement saw the emergence of inspiring leaders like the Ali brothers, Maulana Azad, Maulana Hasrat Mohani, and many others, both men and women. Their collective appeals on religious, political, and social grounds were able to unite Muslims across regions in British India behind the cause of Khilafat.

The movement's integration of religious and political elements helped broaden the base of the Indian independence struggle, making it a key milestone in the fight for self-rule and independence from British colonialism.

KHILAFAT MOVEMENT (1919–24)

Chapter 35:

Non-cooperation Movement (1920)

The Indian National Congress (INC), led by Mahatma Gandhi, began the Non-Cooperation Movement on September 5, 1920. The Non-Cooperation Movement was a nationwide campaign of civil disobedience. Gandhi's philosophy of Satyagraha, which emphasized non-violence and civil resistance, was the driving force behind the movement. The Non-Cooperation Movement is one of the key movements in India's independence struggle. It was initiated by Gandhi in support of the Khilafat Movement. Indians were asked to relinquish their titles and resign from nominated seats in the local bodies as a mark of protest. People were asked to resign from their government jobs. The Non-cooperation movement was based on boycotting British Institutes and commodities like government schools, government offices, courts, and foreign goods. The noncooperation movement was organized by Mahatma Gandhi.

The three main cause behind the Non-Cooperation Movement was:

- Jallianwala Bagh Massacre.

- Rowlatt Act.

- Khilafat Movement.

- Economic Exploitation

- Desire for Swaraj

Many leaders, as well as ordinary individuals, joined the non-cooperation campaign. The Non-Cooperation Movement brought Hindus and Muslims together. Leaders and figures linked with the Non-cooperation Movement include:

Rajendra Prasad, M.N. Roy, Debi Basanti, Sardar Vallabhbhai Patel, Jitendralal Banerjee, Subhash Chandra Bose, Maulana Mohammed Ali, Lala Rai Lajpat

The Non-Cooperation Movement was a defining moment in the Indian independence struggle, marking the first nationwide, nonviolent mass movement. It mobilised millions of Indians, bringing them into the freedom struggle and solidifying Gandhi's role as a national leader. Although it did not achieve Swaraj, it laid the groundwork for future movements. It inspired Indians to believe in their power to challenge colonial rule, underscoring the potential of nonviolent resistance on India's path to independence.

NON-COOPERATION MOVEMENT (1920)

Chapter 36:

The Gudem Rebellion (1920s) – Andhra Pradesh

The Gudem Rebellion, led by **Alluri Sitarama Raju**, was a major uprising against the British in the Gudem Hills of Andhra Pradesh. Alluri Sitarama Raju is one of the unsung heroes of India's freedom movement. He led a guerrilla campaign against the British forces, seeking to defend tribal lands and cultures. The rebellion was primarily sparked by the British imposition of oppressive forest laws that deprived the local tribal people of their natural resources. Though it was eventually crushed, Raju's legacy lives on as a symbol of indigenous resistance.

The Gudem rebellion spread in response to Gandhi's Non-Cooperation Movement. The four features of this rebellion are: In the Gudem Hills of Andhra Pradesh a militant guerrilla movement spread in the early 1920s under the leadership of Alluri Sitaram Raju. The hill people got enraged when the colonial government prevented them from entering the forests to graze their cattle or to collect fuel wood and fruits. They considered Sitaram Raju as an incarnation of God inspired by Gandhiji's Non-Cooperation Movement Raju persuaded the Gudem rebels to wear Khadi and give up drinking. But at the same time he asserted that India could be liberated only by the use of force not non-violence. The Gudem rebels attacked police stations, attempted to kill British officials and carried on guerrilla warfare for achieving Swaraj.

Chapter 37:

Akali Movement (1920–1925)

The Akali movement, also called the Gurdwara Reform Movement, was a campaign to bring reform in the gurdwaras (the Sikh places of worship) in India during the early 1920s. The movement led to the introduction of the Sikh Gurdwara Bill in 1925, which placed all the historical Sikh shrines in India under the control of the Shiromani Gurdwara Parbandhak Committee (SGPC). The Akali Movement (Gurudwara Reform Movement) was initiated by prominent Sikh leaders, including Kartar Singh Jhabbar, who organised non-violent protests, and Baba Kharak Singh, who rallied support for the movement's goals, uniting the Sikh community to regain control of their religious sites.

The Akali Movement played a crucial role in Sikhism and the Indian independence movement, fostering confidence in nonviolent resistance and restoring control of gurdwaras to the Sikh community while strengthening their identity and leading to the Sikh Gurdwara Act of 1925. The Akali Movement instilled confidence in the Indians that the British could be forced to meet their legitimate demands through a nonviolent mass movement. It brought the Akali Dal and the Congress leadership very close to each other, giving a significant boost to the freedom movement in Punjab.

AKALI MOVEMENT (1920-1925)

Chapter 38:

Malabar Rebellion (1921)

The Malabar Rebellion, also known as the Moplah Riots or Moplah Rebellion of 1921 was the culmination of a series of riots by Mappila Muslims of Kerala in the 19th and early 20th centuries against the British and the Hindu landlords in Malabar (Northern Kerala). It was an armed revolt. It was led by Variyamkunnath Kunjahammed Haji.

The Moplah rebellion was sparked by the Khilafat-Non-Cooperation movement. It served as a vehicle for mobilising the Mappilla community, but it had certain conditions under which it was effective. In the same way that not all peasants rose up against the government and landlords, not all Mappillas joined the rebellion. In fact, the rebellion took place predominantly in the Malabar district, where the Khilafat-Non-cooperation movement was least developed in Ernad taluk. As opposed to serving as the end product of mobilisation, the rebellion itself was the driving force behind it. The law required every mappilla in the affected regions to declare allegiance either to the British Raj or to the Khilafat. More people were drawn into the conflict as violence escalated between the two rival polities, making the conflict polarising. As a result of the massive force of official violence, the resistance of the Mappillas was ineffective. By the end of six months, the rebellion had been crushed.

A report by the ICHR-constituted committee (Indian Council of Historical Research) in 2016 has sought the removal of names of 387 'Moplah rioters' (Including leaders Ali Musliyar and Variamkunnath Ahmad Haji) from the list of martyrs.

The Malabar Rebellion (1921) played a significant role in the Indian independence movement by demonstrating the depth of resentment against colonial rule and the socio-economic exploitation of the masses, particularly the peasants. While the rebellion itself was suppressed. It helped to raise political awareness in rural India about the need to resist British colonial policies. It also contributed to the growing nationalist sentiments across India. Although the rebellion was primarily a reaction to local grievances, it highlighted broader themes of anti-colonial resistance and helped lay the groundwork for future uprisings and national movements that would eventually lead to India's independence in 1947.

MALABAR REBELLION, 1921

Chapter 39:

Chauri Chaura Incident (1922)

The Chauri Chaura incident occurred at Chauri Chaura in the Gorakhpur district of the United Province, (modern Uttar Pradesh) in British India on 4 February 1922, when a large group of protesters, participating in the Non-cooperation movement, clashed with police, who opened fire. In retaliation the demonstrators attacked and set fire to a police station, killing all of its occupants. The incident led to the deaths of three civilians and 23 policemen. Mahatma Gandhi, who was strictly against violence, halted the Non-cooperation Movement on the national level on 12 February 1922, as a direct result of this incident

The Chauri Chaura Incident was an unfortunate incident that occured in the Gorakhpur district of Uttar Paresh where local peasants clashed with British policy officials resulting in the death of 22 policemens. Soon after this incident, Mahatma Gandhi who was fairly against violence called off the non-cooperation movement.

The Chauri Chaura incident is significant for highlighting the challenges of maintaining nonviolence in mass movements. It marked a turning point in the Indian freedom struggle, temporarily halting civil disobedience and prompting a rethinking of strategies. It serves as a powerful reminder of the complexities of the independence movement and the critical importance of discipline and nonviolence in achieving political goals.

CHAURI CHAURA INCIDENT (1922)

Chapter 40:

The Rampa Rebellion (1922–1924) – Andhra Pradesh

Manyam, or the Rampa rebellion, was a tribal revolt led by Alluri Sitarama Raju in the Rampa regions of present-day Godavari district in Andhra Pradesh. The uprising was against the exploitative British policies and oppressive forest laws that threatened the lives of tribes in the region.

The rebellion was started by looting police stations in Chintapalli, Krishna Devi Peta, and Rajavommangi by 500 tribals under Raju on August 22, 23, and 24, respectively. The tribal masses showed wholehearted participation throughout the rebellion under Raju, who prepared them and spread the ideals of the non-cooperation movement and Swaraj in the hills. By September, the rebels had defeated the British police five times, and the government dispatched Malabar special police to the hills to put down the rebellion. This forced the rebels to start guerilla warfare, which lasted for two years. Even though the police defeated the villagers at times, they returned to the scene in greater numbers. The government imposed martial law and punitive taxes on the villagers, exerting pressure on them to end the rebellion. A bounty of Rs. 1500 was declared on Raju and Rs. 1000 on Gam Goutham Dora and Gam Mallya Dora, the lieutenants of Raju. Yet the tribal masses continued actively supporting the rebellion, which revealed their deep-rooted anti-British sentiments and yearning for freedom.

Chapter 41:

Kakori Conspiracy (1925)

Kakori Conspiracy also known as The Kakori Train Robbery. It was an armed robbery which took place on August 9, 1925, on a train in central Uttar Pradesh. The robbery occurred at the town of Kakori, about 16 km from Lucknow which was where the train was headed. It involved the looting of government cash from a British train near Kakori, to finance revolutionary activities. The British authorities responded with severe crackdowns, arresting and executing key revolutionaries like Ram Prasad Bismil and Ashfaqulla Khan. This case marked a turning point in the revolutionary movement, inspiring future freedom fighters. The raiders in Kakori Conspiracy were known to be members of the newly formed Hindustan Republican Association, a revolutionary organization, later renamed as Hindustan Socialist Republican Association (HSRA), whose mission was to liberate India from British colonial rule through a revolution which included armed rebellion.

The primary goal of the Kakori Conspiracy Case was to fund the revolutionary activities of the HRA by seizing money that had been collected by the British administration through heavy taxation of Indians. Beyond the monetary aspect, the leaders sought to arouse nationalist sentiment by carrying out a bold and public act of defiance against British rule. The HRA also aimed to garner public attention and create a positive image for their cause.

The Kakori case dealt a significant setback to northern Indian revolutionaries, but it was not a fatal blow. Younger men like Bejoy Kumar Sinha, Shiv Varma, and Jaidev Kapur in Uttar Pradesh, and Bhagat Singh, Bhagwati Charan Vohra, and Sukhdev in Punjab, set out to reorganise the HRA under Chandrashekhar Azad's overall leadership. At the same time, they were being influenced by socialist ideas. Finally, on September 9 and 10, 1928, nearly all of northern India's major young revolutionaries gathered at Feroz Shah Kotla Ground in Delhi, formed a new collective leadership, adopted socialism as their official goal, and renamed the party the Hindustan Socialist Republican Association.

KAKORI CONSPIRACY (1925)

Chapter 42:

The Boycott of the Simon Commission (1927)

Simon Commission was the Indian Statutory Commission, which was a group of seven Members of Parliament under the chairmanship of Sir John Simon. The commission arrived in British India in 1928 to study constitutional reform in Britain's largest and most important possession. The Government of India Act of 1919 provided for the appointment of a commission to study the progress of the governance scheme and suggest new steps after ten years. Since the British administration had failed to include even a single Indian in the Commission, it was strongly opposed by national leaders and freedom. The Simon Commission is also known as the Indian Statutory Commission. It was boycotted by the Indians because:

- All its members were Englishmen

- The Commission had no Indian member

- This was seen as a deliberate insult to the self-respect of the Indians.

- The government showed no inclination towards accepting the demand for Swaraj

- The Commission's report was published in 1930. Before the publication, the government assured that henceforth, Indian opinion would be considered and that the natural outcome of constitutional reforms would be dominion status for India.

- It recommended the abolition of diarchy and the setting-up of representative governments in the provinces.

- It also recommended the retention of separate communal electorates until the communal tensions had died down.

Many consider the Simon Commission as a blessing in disguise. This is because before the Simon Commission matter came to light, Congress was agenda-less. India's opposition to the Simon Commission led Lord Birkenhead to throw an open challenge to the Indian leaders to frame a constitution that would unify the Indian opinion. This challenge was accepted and came out in the form of the Nehru Report, and even though it was not accepted by the younger faction, it was India's first attempt to frame a constitution for its people by its people. The Simon Commission also became the basis of the Government of India Act of 1935.

Simon Commission, group appointed in November 1927 by the British Conservative government under Stanley Baldwin to report on the working of the Indian constitution established by the Government of India Act of 1919

Chapter 43:

Bardoli Satyagraha in Gujarat (1928)

The Bardoli Satyagraha was a significant movement in India led by Sardar Vallabhbhai Patel to oppose the increased taxes imposed by the British government on farmers. It started in June 1928 in Bardoli, Gujarat. The main demand was to cancel a 22% tax hike by the Bombay Presidency.

This movement was crucial in India's fight for independence and was supported by Mahatma Gandhi. It became a strong foundation for the larger Civil Disobedience Movement in 1930. Although Bardoli was initially chosen for the Civil Disobedience Movement, it was later changed due to the Chauri Chaura incident. The Bardoli Satyagraha wanted to have a society where people didn't have to pay taxes. It was a big moment in the fight for India's freedom, even though it didn't focus much on poor farmers or changing the system where people were forced to work. This movement is thought to be a very important part of the Indian Independence Movement.

The Bardoli Satyagraha of 1928 was a significant movement in India's struggle for independence, marked by its profound impact on both the local and national levels. The Satyagraha became a powerful symbol of non-violent resistance against colonial rule, demonstrating Satyagraha's effectiveness in fostering social and political change through truth and non-violence. The movement empowered Bardoli's peasants and inspired agrarian activism across India, emphasising the need to address rural grievances and promoting fair governance. Following the Non-Cooperation Movement, Bardoli emerged as a hub for initiatives like khaddar production, aiding disadvantaged communities and preparing the masses for further agitation.

BARDOLI SATYAGRAHA IN GUJARAT (1928)

The movement was a truly participative and secular peasants movement guided by
SARDAR VALLABHAI PATEL and MOHANDAS KARAMCHAND GANDHI.

Chapter 44:

Hindustan Socialist Republican Association (1928)

The Hindustan Socialist Republican Association (HSRA) was formed on September 10, 1928, at Feroz Shah Kotla, Delhi, by prominent revolutionaries like Chandrashekhar Azad, Bhagat Singh, Sukhdev, Rajguru, Ajay Ghosh, Surya Sen, Jatindranath, and others.

This organisation emerged with the primary aim of establishing a socialist republic in India, marking a shift in revolutionary activity focusing on socialism. HSRA aimed to overthrow British colonial rule through armed struggle inspired by the principles of socialism and equality.

The group is famously known for its acts of defiance, such as the Kakori Train Robbery (1925) and the Lahore Conspiracy Case (1929), which left an indelible mark on India's freedom struggle.

While the revolutionary activities led by the HSRA and the Chittagong Uprising were eventually crushed, their legacy remained a powerful symbol of resistance against British colonial rule. The sacrifices made by these revolutionaries inspired future generations and contributed significantly to the rising tide of nationalism that eventually led to India's independence.

Chapter 45:

Nehru Report (1928) and the Attempt to Draft the Indian Constitution

The Nehru Report was a significant development in the Indian freedom struggle that emerged as a response to the British-imposed Simon Commission, which was criticised for excluding Indian representatives. With no Indian participation in the Commission, Indian leaders took the initiative to present a unified framework for constitutional reforms that would reflect Indian aspirations. This led to the formation of a committee under Motilal Nehru's chairmanship in 1928, and the subsequent proposal became known as the Nehru Report. The report outlined the way forward for India's constitutional future, considering the Indian populace's demands for self-governance and political representation. The Nehru Report had the primary motive of assigning Dominion status to India within the British Commonwealth.

The major components of the Nehru Report are:

- Bill of Rights

- Assigning Equal rights to men and women as citizens

- Formation of a federal form of government with residuary powers in the hands of Centre

- Proposal for the creation of Supreme Court

- This was the first major attempt by Indians to draft a constitution for themselves.

The Nehru Report marked a turning point in India's constitutional history. It highlighted the growing divide within the Indian freedom struggle between those willing to compromise for partial self-rule and those who sought complete independence. It also led to the further development of radical nationalist movements, which would play a crucial role in the coming years as India moved closer to the Civil Disobedience Movement under Mahatma Gandhi.

The Nehru Report was a significant but divisive document in the Indian independence movement. While it offered a detailed vision for India's constitutional future, it failed to address the diverse aspirations of all sections of Indian society. The opposition from key groups, including the Muslim League and radical nationalists, made it clear that the path to Indian self-rule would be complex and fraught with challenges. The Nehru Report remains an important milestone in India's journey toward self-governance, as it demonstrated the growing political maturity of Indian leaders and their commitment to framing an inclusive, democratic constitutional structure for the country.

The Nehru Report of 1928 was a memorandum All Parties Conference in British India to appeal for a new dominion status and a federal set-up of government for the constitution of India

Chapter 46:

Purna Swaraj or Complete Independence Campaign (1929)

The Indian National Congress, on 19 December 1929, passed the historic 'Purna Swaraj' – (total independence) resolution – at its Lahore session. A public declaration was made on 26 January 1930 – a day which the Congress Party urged Indians to celebrate as 'Independence Day'. The declaration was passed due to the breakdown of negotiations between leaders of the freedom movement and the British over the question of dominion status for India. The resolution was a short 750-word document. It did not have a legal/constitutional structure – it read more like a manifesto. It called for severing ties with the British and claimed 'Purna Swaraj' or 'complete independence'. It indicated British rule and succinctly articulated the resulting economic, political and cultural injustice inflicted on Indians. The document spoke on behalf of Indians and made its intention of launching the civil disobedience movement clear.

By recognising the Poorna Swaraj resolution on Constitution Day, India pays homage to the transformative power of this historic moment. It serves as a powerful reminder of the unyielding determination of the Indian people to break free from the chains of colonial rule and assert their right to self-governance. The resolution symbolises the collective will of the nation and reflects the indomitable spirit that propelled the freedom movement forward. Constitution Day provides a platform to reflect on the foundational role that the Poorna Swaraj resolution played in shaping the future of India. It signifies the commitment to building a nation that is based on democratic principles, upholds the values of freedom and justice, and ensures equality for all its citizens. The recognition of this resolution within the constitutional framework highlights its enduring relevance and affirms its place in the nation's historical narrative.

Constitution Day serves as an opportunity to educate and inspire future generations about the sacrifices and struggles that were endured in the pursuit of independence.By commemorating this day, India reaffirms its dedication to upholding the principles and aspirations enshrined in the resolution, fostering a sense of unity and shared purpose among its citizens. The Poorna Swaraj resolution holds immense historical and symbolic importance within the context of British India. Its recognition on Constitution Day during the constitution-making period amplifies its lasting relevance and the foundational role it played in shaping India's path towards complete independence. This resolution continues to serve as a powerful reminder of the ideals and aspirations that guide the nation as it strives for progress, unity, and the fulfilment of the vision encapsulated within the Poorna Swaraj resolution.

The word Purna Swaraj was derived from Sanskrit पूर्ण (Pūrṇa) 'Complete', and स्वराज (Svarāja or Swarāj) 'Self-rule or Sovereignty', or Declaration of the Independence of India

Chapter 47:

Jinnah's 14 Point Programme (1929)

Jinnah's 14 Points were a set of demands for constitutional reform and political rights for Muslims in India. They were proposed by Muhammad Ali Jinnah in response to the Nehru Report (1928). These demands included four Delhi proposals, three Calcutta amendments, separate electorates, and reservation of seats for Muslims in government services and self-governing bodies. Jinnah's primary goal was to protect Muslim interests. Jinnah's 14 Points became the core demands of the Muslim League, significantly shaping political thought henceforth and eventually leading to the creation of Pakistan.

Jinnah's Fourteen Points programme (1929)

- Federal constitution with residual powers with the provinces.

- Provincial autonomy.

- No constitutional amendment without the agreement of the states.

- All legislatures and elected bodies to have adequate Muslim representation without reducing Muslim majority in a province to minority or equality.

- Adequate Muslim representation of Muslims in the services and in self-governing bodies.

- 1/3rd representation of Muslims in the Central Legislature.

- 1/3rd Muslim members in the central and state cabinets.

- Separate electorates.

- No bill to be passed in any legislature if 3/4th of a minority community considers it against its interests.

- Any reorganisation of territories not to affect the Muslim majority in Bengal, Punjab and the NWFP.

- Separation of Sindh from Bombay Presidency.

- Constitutional reforms in the NWFP and Baluchistan.

- Full religious freedom for all communities.

- Protection of the religious, cultural, educational and language rights of Muslims.

Jinnah's 14-Point Program (1930) marked a critical moment in the history of the Indian independence movement, as it articulated the demands of Indian Muslims for political safeguards, autonomy, and representation. These points not only shaped the future course of the Muslim League's political strategy but also deepened the divisions between Hindus and Muslims within the broader Indian nationalist struggle. While the INC was focused on achieving Indian unity, the 14 Points foreshadowed the Muslim League's eventual demand for Pakistan, setting the stage for the partition of India in 1947.

JINNAH'S 14 POINT PROGRAMME (1930)

The Fourteen Points of Jinnah were proposed by
Muhammad Ali Jinnah in response to the Nehru report

Chapter 48:

Khudai Khidmatgar Movement (1929–1947)

In 1929, the Khudai Khidmatgars ("Servants of God") movement, led by Khan Abdul Ghaffar Khan, nonviolently mobilized to oppose the British in India's North West Frontier Province. Ghaffar Khan and the Khudai Khidmatgar movement inspired thousands of Pashtuns (also called Pathans), who were known as fierce warriors, and others to lay down their arms and use civil resistance to challenge British rule. Although Ghaffar Khan's initial reform efforts predated his involvement with Gandhi and the Indian National Congress (INC), he later formed a formal alliance with them and became a formidable force during and following the INC's civil disobedience campaign of 1930-1931, helping the INC win provincial elections in 1937.

Ghaffar Khan, who is also known as Badshah Khan and the "Frontier Gandhi," formed the world's first nonviolent army, a force of perhaps 100,000 Pathans who took a solemn oath in joining the "Servants of God" movement. The Khudai Khidmatgar movement was highly organized with both democratic councils, on the one hand, and a military-like activist wing that employed a wide variety of nonviolent strategic actions in their civil resistance to British rule.

The Khudai Khidmatgar campaign succeeded in educating Indians on the necessary nonviolent tactics to reform society so that, in time, the British could be ousted from India. The campaign was also successful in achieving several short-term goals, such as increased government finance for education, health, agriculture, and veterinary medicine. In 1932, the government brought the Frontier Province to the same level of administration as other parts of India, and urban and rural elections followed shortly thereafter. In 1934 after negotiations between Gandhi and the British government resulted in Britain conceding other immediate Indian demands in India, the Indian National Congress ended the campaign, which was nicknamed "the Salt Satyagraha." Gandhi launched other campaigns before independence was achieved in 1947.

Khudai Khidmatgar

Chapter 49:

The Meerut Conspiracy Case (1929)

The Meerut Conspiracy Case was a controversial court case during British colonial rule. This case involved a group of Indian trade unionists and communist leaders accused of plotting to overthrow the British government in India. The trial, which began in 1929, revealed the British political machinations and the growing unrest and demand for workers' rights and political freedom.

The Meerut Conspiracy Case (1929) is significant in the history of India's national liberation struggle. It occurred when the entire capitalist world was reeling from the Great Depression while the newly formed socialist state of Soviet Russia was making tremendous progress. During this time, militant working-class struggles, most of which were led by communists and revolutionaries, reached new heights. Prominent leaders involved in the Meerut Conspiracy Case were Shripad Amrut Dange, Muzaffar Ahmed and Keshav Neelkanth Joglekar. The Meerut Conspiracy Case (1929-1933) led to 27 convictions, severe sentences, and later appeals, resulting in reduced penalties and acquittals for the remaining defendants.

The Meerut Conspiracy Case (1929) played an important role in the Indian independence struggle by highlighting the rising revolutionary sentiment and the repressive nature of British colonial rule. While the case did not result in an immediate shift in British policies, it significantly contributed to the growing divisions within the Indian nationalist movement and demonstrated the determination of the revolutionaries to pursue independence through radical means. The trial and subsequent repression led to increased public support for revolutionary groups and inspired future leaders, such as Bhagat Singh, who would become central figures in the broader struggle for independence.

M.N. Roy after release from jail, welcomed by K.F. Nariman, Maniben Kara, Yousuf Mehrali, Leelavathi Munshi (1936)

Chapter 50:

Salt March or Dandi March (1930)

The Salt March was one of the most famous early acts of civil disobedience, led by nonviolence leader Mahatma Gandhi as part of India's protest to gain freedom from the British. In 1882, the British government implemented the Salt Act which prohibited Indians from collecting or selling salt, forcing them to buy salt from the British instead. This gave the British a monopoly on the good. The Indians were forced to incur a heavy salt tax charged by British sellers, especially since salt was a staple in their diet. To protest this law, Gandhi declared resistance to the Salt Act and started a campaign of mass civil disobedience, or 'satyagraha'.

Initially, Gandhi's idea of using salt as the centerpiece of their protest led to reluctance from the rest of the activists. It seemed like such a small thing to focus on in the midst of the national struggle. However, Gandhi reasoned that they needed something to unite people of different classes and backgrounds, and salt was the answer. Salt was a daily necessity for most Indians, and the salt tax had hurt all of them immensely. He also felt that a common factor was needed to unite the Muslims and Hindus to revolt against the British by fighting something that impacted both groups. Thus, the idea of the Salt March began to take place.

In 1930, Gandhi and 79 of his followers left Sabarmati Ashram to walk through Gujarat to the coastal town of Dandi with the intention of producing salt. During the 24 days of the march he spoke to thousands of people and led prayers, convincing many more to join the trail. When he reached Dandi, he planned to work the salt flats on the beach but the police had crushed the salt deposits into the mud. Nevertheless, he reached down and picked up a small lump of natural salt out of the mud as an act of defiance towards the British. Thousands of people in the other coastal cities followed Gandhi by making salt on their own, disrupting the British's order.

SALT MARCH (1930)

The Salt March, also known as the Salt Satyagraha, Dandi March and the Dandi Satyagraha, was an act of nonviolent civil disobedience in colonial India led by Mahatma Gandhi

Chapter 51:

Civil Disobedience Movement (1930)

The Civil Disobedience Movement was launched after the observance of Independence Day in 1930. By 1930, the Congress Party had announced that the only goal of the liberation movement should be Poorna Swaraj or total independence. The 26 January 1930 was declared Poorna Swaraj Day. The movement began in 1930 after Indians became angered when the British imposed a tax on the sale and collection of salt, and Gandhiji chose to break the salt tax in defiance of the government. More than 60,000 individuals were detained as the movement swept across the nation, including Mahatma Gandhi. The primary factors that contributed to the conditions for the Civil Disobedience Movement included protests against the arrest of revolutionary leaders, India's pursuit of its own constitution, and a growing demand for complete independence following the rejection of Dominion status as proposed in the Nehru Report.

Prominent leaders like Sarojini Naidu started emerging, and their involvement marked a change in women's active participation in the freedom struggle. The British responded by repression, mass arrests drew international attention to the Indian struggle for independence. The movement led to the Gandhi-Irwin Pact in 1931, when the British agreed to some concessions and Gandhi agreed to suspend the movement. The movement promoted national unity and public mobilization against British rule across the country, thus strengthening collective Indian resolve for independence. The Civil Disobedience Movement set the example of non-violent resistance across the globe and was a vital step towards India's ultimate independence in 1947.

Despite not achieving its goals of Purna Swaraj, the Movement occupies a special place in the history of India's quest for freedom. Congress could mobilise great political support and got moral authority that was reflected in the massive victory in the 1937 election. The resolution of Purna Swaraj and its attributes, declared in the Karachi Resolution, shows the drifting of Congress towards greater radicalisation.

CIVIL DISOBEDIENCE MOVEMENT (1930)

The civil disobedience movement was a landmark event in the Indian Nationalist movement. In many ways, the movement is credited for paving the way for freedom in India.

Chapter 52:

The First Round Table Conferences (1930), Second Round Table Conference (1931) & Third Round Table Conference (1932)

The Round Table Conferences held between 1930 and 1932, were a series of high-profile discussions organised by the British government to frame a constitutional future for India.

These conferences became a platform to negotiate between Indian political aspirations and British colonial policies.

The First Round Table Conference was conducted from November 12, 1930, to January 19, 1931. The Congress boycotted the meeting as the British government refused to consider the Congress's demand for Poorna Swaraj. The first Round Table Conference convened by Labour Government Prime Minister Ramsay McDonald. The issue discussed were proposed Federal government, constitution of the province, Minorities Defence Services in Sindh and NWFP Provinces,proposed separate electorates for the 'untouchables',issues related to Burma, the notion of an All-India Federation.

The Second Round Table Conference was held in London from 7 September 1931 to 1 December 1931 with the participation of Gandhi and the Indian National Congress. The session started on 7 September 1931. The major difference between the first and the second conference was that the INC was participating in the second one. This was one of the results of the Gandhi-Irwin Pact. Another difference was that unlike the previous time, British PM Macdonald was heading not a Labour government, but a National government. The Labour Party had been toppled two weeks before in Britain.

The third Round Table Conference took place between 17 November 1932 and 24 December 1932. Only 46 delegates in total took part in this conference. Indian princely states were represented by princes and divans. British Indians were represented by the Aga Khan (Muslims), women, Europeans, Anglo-Indians and labour groups also attended. The recommendations of this conference were published in a White Paper in 1933 and later discussed in the British Parliament. The recommendations were analysed, and the Government of India Act of 1935 was passed on its basis.

These conferences highlighted the deep divisions between various Indian groups and the British government. The constitutional deliberations laid the groundwork for the Government of India Act of 1935, which introduced limited provincial autonomy but fell short of Indian aspirations for self-rule.

THE FIRST ROUND TABLE CONFERENCE (1930)

First Round Table Conference (November 1930 – January 1931) The Round Table Conference officially inaugurated by His Majesty George V on November 12, 1930 in Royal Gallery House of Lords at London and chaired by the Prime Minister.

SECOND ROUND TABLE CONFERENCE (1931)

The culmination of events were settled by the Gandhi–Irwin Pact (1931).
A chastised Gandhi wanted the peaceful end to civil disobedience demanded
by the Viceroy and his Council.

Chapter 53:

Trial of Bhagat Singh, Rajguru and Sukhdev. (1930)/Lahore Conspiracy Case

The Lahore Conspiracy Case was a significant event in India's freedom struggle, involving Bhagat Singh and his revolutionary comrades from the Hindustan Socialist Republican Association. Following the killing of British officer J.P. Saunders in retaliation for the death of Lala Lajpat Rai, Bhagat Singh and associates were arrested, igniting widespread protests against British rule. During the trial, Bhagat Singh and his comrades undertook a hunger strike to demand recognition as political prisoners. Although the Lahore Conspiracy Case trial resulted in the execution of Bhagat Singh, Rajguru, and Sukhdev, it emerged as a potent symbol of resistance against British rule.

The 1915 Lahore Conspiracy Case involved trials related to the Ghadar conspiracy, held in Lahore and the U.S. from April to September under a special tribunal established by the Defence of India Act. Of the 291 convicted, 42 were executed, 114 received life sentences, 93 got various prison terms, and 42 were acquitted. Kartar Singh Sarabha was executed for his role in the conspiracy.

The trials for the Lahore Conspiracy Case attracted significant public attention and faced criticism, with allegations of being politically motivated and lacking due process. It Began in June 1930 and concluded in October 1930. Bhagat Singh, Sukhdev, and Rajguru were charged for their roles in the bombing and Saunders' murder. The court convicted them and sentenced them to death by hanging. Other individuals received varying prison terms. The death sentences sparked widespread protests across India. Bhagat Singh, Sukhdev, and Rajguru were executed on March 23, 1931.

Chapter 54:

The Naga Nationalist Movement, (1930)

Haipou Jadonang, a Rongmei Naga leader (one of the major indigenous Naga tribes of North-East India) from Manipur, was a spiritual and political leader who fought for freedom from the clutches of British colonial rule. He began establishing an army, Riphen, that comprised 500 men and women who were well trained in military tactics, weaponry and reconnaissance missions. Besides these activities, the recruits assisted in civilian matters such as farming. He was arrested in 1931 and hanged by the colonial rulers.

Among the Naga ethnic groups in Manipur, it was the Zeliangrong Nagas who took the initiative to revolt against British rule in Manipur. This movement can be considered as the early political movement of the Nagas. It was led by the charismatic leaders, Haipou Jadonang and his cousin sister Rani Gaidinliu. Jadonang, who declared himself as the 'messiah king" was born in the year 1905 at Kambiron (Puilon) village in Tamenglong district of Manipur.

While the Naga Nationalist Movement was not directly connected to the Indian National Congress or the mainstream nationalist struggle, it was still part of the larger wave of anti-colonial resistance against British rule. The Naga people's desire for autonomy mirrored similar demands for self-rule across India. The Naga movement, though not fully recognized by other Indian nationalist groups, contributed to the broader conversation on the rights of indigenous groups and ethnic minorities within India. The demand for self-rule and independence by the Naga people also challenged the British assumption that all communities in India would be satisfied with being part of a united India under British rule. It was one of the earliest instances of ethnic separatism and self-determination that would surface again in the Indian subcontinent in the decades to come.

The Naga Nationalist Movement (1930) was a significant early expression of Naga political identity and resistance to colonial rule. Although the movement was not as widely recognized or as influential in the mainstream Indian independence struggle as movements led by the Indian National Congress, it played a crucial role in the political development of the Naga people. The movement contributed to the broader anti-colonial struggle by asserting the rights of ethnic minorities and highlighting the complexities of India's diverse identity. The Naga people's demand for self-determination and independence continues to have a lasting impact on India's northeastern politics, with the Naga peace process still ongoing.

Chapter 55:

Karachi Session of INC (1931)

The historical Karachi Session of Congress in 1931 was presided by Sardar Vallabhbhai Patel. The Karachi Congress Session in 1931, was held following the Gandhi–Irwin Pact and in the immediate aftermath of Bhagat Singh's execution. As a result, throughout Gandhi's route to Karachi, he was greeted with black flag demonstrations by the Punjab Naujawan Bharat Sabha, in protest against his failure to secure commutation of the death sentence for Bhagat and his comrades. The Karachi session is memorable for a resolution on Fundamental Rights and the National Economic Programme. The resolution guaranteed basic civil and political rights to the people. The Karachi Session of the Indian National Congress, held in 1931, adopted the famous resolution outlining the shape of independent India's Constitution. Some basic values, like universal adult franchise, the right to freedom and equality, and protection of the rights of the minorities, were accepted by all leaders. Though the Foundation of Indian National Congress (INC) was in 1885, it stands as a cornerstone in India's fight for independence and has played a crucial role in shaping the country's political landscape. Before its inception, several socio-political movements and organizations laid the groundwork for the formation of the Indian National Congress. Till 1947, there were numerous INC sessions (annual and special INC sessions) to discuss the political situation in the country and to pass resolutions on important issues. These INC sessions served as platforms for inclusive and collective decision-making and planning for the course of India's struggle for freedom. Foundation of the Indian National Congress. While many Indians had been contemplating the formation of an all-India organization for nationalist political activists, it was A.O. Hume, a retired English Civil Servant, who played a crucial role in giving the idea a concrete and definitive form. He engaged with prominent Indian leaders and collaborated with them to organize the inaugural INC session in Bombay in December 1885.

The socio-economic provision in the Karachi Resolution went on to influence the Constituent Assembly in drawing up Part IV of the Indian Constitution – the Directive Principles of State Policy. The Karachi Congress met at a time when Gandhi called a 'truce' with the British government to negotiate a pact with the Viceroy, Lord Irwin, in February 1931.

The primary agenda for the Karachi Congress was to ratify the Gandhi-Irwin Pact, which was greatly criticised by nationalists for its compromising nature. The enlightened vision of the session, guided the Congress in later years. When ministries were formed in 1937 by Congress in various provinces, they tried to execute some of them like legalising trade unions, land reforms (partial though), press freedom etc. The influence of this resolution can also be found in the formation and recommendation of National Planning committee headed by Subhash Chandra Bose (1938)

KARACHI SESSION OF INC (1931)

Chapter 56:

Gandhi-Irwin Pact (1931)

Gandhi-Irwin Pact is the name given to a political agreement concluded by Mahatma Gandhi and Lord Irwin, the then Viceroy of India, on 5th March 1931. The Indian National Congress (INC) agreed to take part in the Round Table Conference. The government agreed to withdraw all ordinances, revoke the ban on the INC, restore the confiscated properties of the Satyagrahis, and also agreed to permit the collection of salt by people near the sea coasts.

It marked the end of a period of civil disobedience (satyagraha) in India against British rule that Gandhi and his followers had initiated with the Salt March (March–April 1930).Many British officials in India, and in Great Britain, were outraged by the idea of a pact with a party, whose avowed purpose was the destruction of the British Raj. Despite boycotting the first Round Table Conference, members of the CWC attended the second conference in September 1931.

Further, Bans on the INC were lifted, and it was permitted to hold peaceful meetings that were not intended to be anti-establishment. As a significant fact, this was the second high-level meeting between Gandhi and a Viceroy in 13 years after the initiation of the Montagu–Chelmsford Reforms in 1919.

GANDHI-IRWIN PACT (1931)

Chapter 57:

The Communal Award (1932)

The Communal Award (also known as MacDonald Award) was created by the British prime minister Ramsay MacDonald on 16 August 1932; and was announced after the Round Table Conference (1930–32). The Communal Award, based on the findings of the Indian Franchise Committee (also called the Lothian Committee), established separate electorates and reserved seats for minorities, including the depressed classes which were granted seventy-eight reserved seats.

During the late 19th and early 20th centuries, the awareness among the oppressed sections of society increased. They began to raise their voices against the violation of rights and social equality in the country. The British government initiated the constitutional reforms under pressure from the Indian national movement to accommodate Indians in multiple representative bodies. When the separate electorate was formed for Muslims under the Morley – Minto Reforms Act of 1909, leaders of the less privileged sections decided to raise their voices and demand seat reservations. After many revolts, the depressed class forced the British government to get an invitation for their representative to the round table conference in London. However, the Congress party and Gandhi both were not on the same page as they were not satisfied with the idea of demanding a separate electorate. During this time, BR Ambedkar evolved as a strong supporter for the rights of the deprived sections and attacked Congress for not addressing their issues.

In simple terms, the communal award is a set of elections awarded to the less privileged or the downtrodden sections of society. During the late 19th and early 20th centuries, the awareness among the depressed section of society started to increase. They raised their voices against the violation of rights and social equality in the country.

THE COMMUNAL AWARD (1932)

Chapter 58:

Poona Pact (1932)

The Poona Pact was an agreement between M K Gandhi and B R Ambedkar signed in the Yerwada Central Jail, Poona on September 24th, 1932 on behalf of the depressed class for the reservation of the electoral seats in the Legislature of the British Government.

It was signed by Ambedkar on behalf of the depressed classes and by Madan Mohan Malviya on behalf of Hindus and Gandhi as a means to end the fast that Gandhi was undertaking in jail as a protest against the decision made by British Prime Minister Ramsay MacDonald to give separate electorates to depressed classes for the election of members of provincial legislative assemblies in British India. The Poona Pact of 1932 was significant as it replaced the divisive Communal Award, offering reserved seats for the Depressed Classes within the general electorate. This compromise, negotiated between Gandhi and Ambedkar, ensured greater political representation for the marginalised group, promoting unity and addressing their long-standing grievances.

POONA PACT (1932)

Chapter 59:

Government of India Act (1935)

The Government of India Act (1935) was an important constitutional reform that aimed to introduce limited self-government in British India. It established provincial autonomy and expanded legislative councils, although power remained primarily in British hands.

The Government of India Act of 1935, introduced a federal system at the centre, aimed at dividing powers between the central government and the provinces. The federal system was meant to be a compromise, offering more autonomy to the provinces, but its success could have been improved. It was primarily designed to ensure British control over India's governance, with the ultimate authority resting with the British Crown.

In conclusion, the Government of India Act, 1935, represented a step toward constitutional reform in India but fell short of meeting the demands for full self-rule. Despite its limitations, it played a crucial role in shaping the constitutional framework that would eventually lead to the creation of independent India in 1947.

GOVERNMENT OF INDIA ACT (1935)

Chapter 60:

Resignation of Congress Ministries (1939)

The Congress ministries resigned in October and November 1939, in protest against Viceroy Lord Linlithgow's action of dragging India into the Second World War without the consent of her people. There was malicious propaganda carried out against the Congress by the Communal parties. They accused the Congress of discrimination against the minorities, but such propaganda was carried out due to political and communal overtones, rather than on factual basis. At this time, many opportunists joined the Congress during this period in order to seek advantages of office. Congress was aware of such characters, and Gandhi wrote frankly about corruption in the Congress in his paper Harijan. During this period, the Congress held two sessions. The Fifty First session was held at **Haripura** in February, 1938 under the presidency of Subhas Chandra Bose. This session passed a number of resolutions related to international affairs as well as on the internal situation in India. It was at the next session (Tripuri) that the Congress faced a major crisis. This time an election was held for the President and Bose defeated Pattabhi Sitaramayya by 1580 to 1377 votes.

Viceroy Linlithgow declared India at war with Britain in 1939. The Congress objected strongly to the declaration of war without prior consultation with Indians.The Congress Working Committee suggested that it would cooperate if there a central Indian national government were formed, and a commitment were made to India's independence after the war. The government did not come up with any satisfactory response. As a result, the Congress Ministries resigned office in November, 1939 on the ground that the Viceroy on its own had made India a participant in the imperialist war without consulting the Congress. Eventually, the Muslim League under Jinnah celebrated this as 'deliverance day' whereas the nationalists stood behind the Congress and the subsequent events led to the Individual Satyagraha in 1900 and the Quit India movement in 1942, besides Bose going aboard and leading the Azad Hind Fauj.

Chapter 61:

Crisis at Tripuri (1939)

The Tripuri Session of the Indian National Congress (1939) was important in modern Indian history because it was marked by internal strife between the Congress members and also a resolution reiterating Gandhiji's leadership was moved by Govind Ballabh Pant.

The Tripuri Session of the Indian National Congress presided over by Subhas Chandra Bose marked a crucial milestone in the history of the Indian national movement. This session, which was held in the present-day Jabalpur district of Madhya Pradesh, witnessed the passage of a critical resolution that facilitated the integration of the political struggle in the princely states and the rest of India. The Civil Disobedience Movement saw the spread of the nationalist creed across the nation, even in places which had been politically dormant previously. The 1930s in particular witnessed considerable political activity and turbulence in the Princely States across the nation from Jaipur to Rajkot. In view of this widespread political awakening Mahatma Gandhi and Sardar Patel, who had previously advocated in favour of a policy of non-intervention in these regions, changed their stance, and exhorted the Congress to endorse their political movements. Their advice was accepted at the Tripuri Session, which adopted a resolution stating that it was abandoning its previous policy of non-interference in the struggle in the princely states. The resolution asserted: "The Congress desires to reiterate that its objective, Complete Independence, is for the whole of India, inclusive of the States, which are integral parts of India…"

On the heels of the Tripuri Session, the Ludhiana Session of the All India State's People's Conference was held, where Jawaharlal Nehru accepted the Presidency of the organization. Hereon, the Praja Mandals worked in close coordination with the Congress to fight for Indian Independence in a united manner.

CRISIS OF TRIPURI (1939)

Chapter 62:

The August Offer (1940)

The August Offer was made by Lord Linlithgow, Viceroy of India, in August 1940. It is known as 'The August Offer' since it was presented in the month of August. The viceroy Linlithgow made the August Offer promising to establish an advisory war council, to expand and include more Indians in the Viceroy Executive Council, and to set up a representative Indian body to frame the Constitution of India. It was rejected on the fact that the Britishers were not guaranteeing their complete sovereignty and just the Dominion Status for the country.

The British government made an August offer to gain India's support in World War II. France, Britain's close ally, had collapsed and been occupied by the Nazis during the war. As a result, the British required India's participation in the war. The August Offer, however, was rejected by Indian leaders. Gandhiji launched a limited 'Individual Satyagraha' in response to the August Offer. It was a protest against the British government and their inability to meet Indian demands.

THE AUGUST OFFER (1940)

Chapter 63:

Individual Satyagraha (1940)

Individual Satyagraha was the resultant of August offer. It was started with the mass Civil Disobedience Movement by M.K Gandhi on Individual Satyagraha. This was a movement for not only to seek independence but also to affirm the right of Speech. The demand of the Satyagrahi was using freedom of Speech against the war through an anti-war declaration. If the government does not arrest the Satyagrahi, he or she will repeat it in villages and start a march towards Delhi ("Delhi Chalo Movement").

The leaders of the Indian National Congress (INC) were unhappy with the British government for dragging India into the Second World War in 1939, without the Indian people's consent. Indian backing for the war was highly desired by the British government and as a result, the Viceroy Linlithgow offered a series of recommendations known as the "August offer."After the Indian nationalists demanded an interim government in India in lieu of support in World War II, Indians' freedom to frame their own constitution was acknowledged for the first time in the August Offer, 1940. The August Offer said after the war, a representative Indian body would be established to draft India's Constitution, and it would be given dominion status. The INC rejected this offer at its meeting at Wardha in August 1940 and demanded complete freedom from colonial rule. The Individual Satyagraha was then started by Mahatma Gandhi to uphold the right to free expression. Brahma Datt, Vinoba Bhave and Jawaharlal Nehru were the first three satyagrahis. The satyagrahis also started a march towards Delhi, which was called the 'Delhi Chalo Movement'. Although the movement failed to pick up steam and was aborted in December 1940, it put the Britishers under immense pressure.

The Individual Satyagraha movement provided a platform for the ordinary people to express their dissent against British policies at a personal level. It was a unique form of resistance that emphasised the power of one's individuality in the larger politics of the freedom struggle.

INDIVIDUAL SATYAGRAHA (1940)

Chapter 64:

Cripps Mission (1942)

The threat of the Japanese invading India was increasing with passing the time as they were advancing outside the Indian eastern borders; however, the support of India was exceptionally crucial for Britain's war efforts. In 1939, when the second world war broke out, India was declared as a party to the war as part of the British Empire by the Viceroy Lord Linlithgow. Since it was done without any consultations, it broke into massive protests, especially from one of India's biggest parties of that time, the congress. The party leaders decided to resign from their respective posts, which was also celebrated as Deliverance Day' by the Muslim league.

Britain started to feel immense pressure in regards to its own imperial policies from the US and several other aligned forces. This was marked as the arrival of Cripps mission as the British government sent Cripps to India. Stafford Cripps, along with Lord Privy Seal, headed the Cripps Mission. There were other members as well who played a significant role. It includes the leader of the House of Common, and so on. Starting in 1942, the Cripps Mission was a failed attempt made by the British government. The mission was headed by a member of the War Cabinet, Stafford Cripps, who was sent to India from March 22 to April 11, 1942. As this mission was not successful, the issue of the constitution of India was postponed for some time. The arrival of Cripps mission was on March 22 in Delhi.

It was during the Cripps Mission when the British government acknowledged the right to be a dominion for India. Indians have the power to frame their own constitution . During the interim period, Indians were promised a greater share in administrative decisions.

In March 1942, The Cripps Mission was sent to India by the British government for obtaining Indian cooperation for the British war efforts in the 2nd World War. Sir Richard Stafford Cripps headed the Cripps Mission. Although Cripps Mission brought several massive changes, it was called off as the proposals were seen as too radical and too conservative.

The Cripps Mission (1942) played a crucial role in the Indian independence movement by exposing the irreconcilable differences between Indian leaders and the British. The failure of the mission intensified the demand for immediate independence, led to the Quit India Movement, and deepened the divisions between the Indian National Congress and the Muslim League. While it did not lead to any immediate concessions, the mission's failure hastened the end of British rule in India and set the stage for the eventual partition and independence of India in 1947.

CRIPPS MISSION (1942)

Chapter 65:

Quit India Movement (1942)

Quit India Movement was a massive anti-colonial struggle in India, launched on August 8, 1942, under the leadership of Mahatma Gandhi, who gave the mantra of "Do or Die" during this Movement. Projected initially as the civil disobedience movement, this 'third great wave' of India's struggle for freedom soon took a violent turn with the aim of 'fight to the finish' of the colonial empire. Gandhi, understanding the mood of the nation and the importance of individual liberties, was even prepared for riots and violence caused by the Quit India Movement as he thought it morally correct to defend against the state's organised violence.

The Quit India Movement gained support from leaders from all over the country. However, the Communist Party of India, the Hindu Mahasabha and the India Muslim league did not support the movement. The Communist Party did not support the mission because of the deep-rooted association of communism with the then Soviet Union and hence the inherent support towards World War II. The Hindu Mahasabha did not support the movement for fear of the nation's safety and security during such a dire situation. The Muslim League did not support the movement, as it wished for the formation of a separate country before India got complete freedom. Some important leaders of the Quit India Movement were Mahatma Gandhi, Jawahar Lal Nehru, Maulana Abul Kalam Azad, Subhash Chandra Bose, Biju Patnaik, Aruna Asaf Ali, Ram Manohar Lohia, Usha Mehta, Sucheta Kriplani and Jai Prakash Narain. Subhash Chandra Bose formed the Indian National Army and fought for absolute freedom during this time. Subhash Chandra Bose contributed from outside the country.

Strikes and rallies were held around the country, and workers showed their solidarity by refusing to work in the factories. It was a phase marked by urban insurrection with strikes, bans and protests, all of which were soon put down. To suppress the movement, Gandhi was arrested and imprisoned at the Aga Khan Palace in Pune, and nearly all the movement's leaders were arrested in this phase. In the second phase, the focus switched to the rural areas with significant revolts. This phase saw rampant destruction of communication systems such as railway tracks and stations, telegraph cables and poles and attacks on government buildings and other obvious symbols of the British administration. The third phase of the movement was marked by the formation of local government at different levels, depicting the people's acceptance of authority figures.

Following WWII, Britain's global stature had transformed considerably, and the clamour for independence could no longer be ignored. Above all, the Quit India Movement united the Indians against British rule. Although most protests had been put down by 1944, Gandhi continued to struggle and went on a 21-day fast upon his release. The Quit India Movement ignited the spark in the struggle for freedom and is regarded as one of the most crucial movements in India's struggle for independence.

QUIT INDIA MOVEMENT (1942)

Chapter 66:

Azad Hind Fauz (1942)

Azad Hind Fauj or the India National Army (INA) was first established by Mohan Singh in 1942. It was revived by Netaji Subhas Chandra Bose on October 21, 1943, during the Second World War to secure India's complete independence from British Raj. Hence, every year on 21 October, the anniversary of the formation of Azad Hind Government is celebrated across the country. On this day, India's first independent provisional government named Azad Hind Government was announced.

Major operations of the Azad Hind Fauj (Indian National Army):

Arakan Campaign (January–February 1944)

The INA participated in its first major operation, the Arakan Campaign. It was a part of the Japanese U-Go offensive into India. The INA achieved initial success, capturing the town of Mowdok. It was eventually forced to withdraw due to heavy British resistance and Japanese logistical failures.

Imphal–Kohima Campaign (March–June 1944)

The INA played a major role in the Imphal–Kohima Campaign, the largest Japanese offensive of World War II. The INA fought alongside Japanese forces in an attempt to capture the important towns of Imphal and Kohima. However, it was ultimately defeated by the British. The campaign was a major turning point in the war in Asia, and the INA suffered heavy casualties.

Burma Campaign (1944–1945)

The INA continued to fight alongside the Japanese in Burma until the end of the war. The INA fought in several battles during this period. This included the Battle of Irrawaddy River and the Battle of Mount Popa.

Indian National Army was a group with a variety of objectives. Its purpose was to bolster and fill out Japanese claims of establishing a Greater Asia co-prosperity zone. The INA was also formed to promote the development of armed Indian nationalism. It was created to weaken the British Indian Army, which was the backbone of British imperial power in the Far East. The military participation of the INA was insignificant. On the Burma-India border, the army fought one significant battle, the Battle of Imphal-Kohima, but was beaten piecemeal. Its contribution to the cause of Indian nationalism, on the other hand, was far from insignificant. The British colonial administration planned to try the remaining members of the INA for treason. The fact that the trials would be held at the Red Fort sparked a fresh wave of nationalism in the country, as the Indian populace regarded the members as patriots fighting for freedom. The trials brought the British into nothing short of an imperial dilemma. The trial also resulted in a rebellion inside the UK Indian Army, with the Royal Indian Navy being particularly prominent. This led the British to understand that they had lost the military's backing, and so their departure from India was inevitable.

AZAD HIND FAUZ (1942)

Chapter 67:

Simla Conference & The Wavell Plan (1945)

The Wavell Plan was first presented at the Simla Conference in 1945. It was named after the Viceroy of India, Lord Wavell.

The Shimla Conference was convened in order to agree on the Wavell Plan for Indian self-government, which provided for separate representations on communal lines. Both the plan and the conference failed on account of the Muslim League and the Indian National Congress not coming to an agreement. Lord Wavell invited 21 political leaders including Mahatma Gandhi and M A Jinnah to Shimla, the summer capital of British India to discuss the Wavell Plan on June 25th, 1945.

At a conference convened at British India's summer capital, Shimla, in 1945, representatives of renowned activists from the Indian freedom movement attended from each community or political organisation. The Shimla Conference consisted of debates between men who held strong views about their respective communities, ideologies, and the role they would play after the Queen's government left India. It was not a productive conference, but it provided a platform for attendees to further articulate their demands or demands as to their level of representation post-independence. Thus, the conference did not achieve its desired outcome.

Wavell's Plan was established to resolve the political deadlock in India, but he abandoned the proposals due to disputes between Muslim League leaders and Congress leaders, and eventually, the proposals were thrown out at the Simla Conference. With the end of the world war and the Labour Party taking power, Wavell's efforts had come to a halt. Labour Party leaders wanted India's independence as soon as possible, so they sent a cabinet mission to accomplish this exact goal. A major cause of the partition of India is viewed as the Simla Conference. Ultimately, partition was inevitable because of Jinnah's adamant stance in favour of a separate Muslim state and the INC's resistance to nominating Muslim representatives.

Chapter 68:

INA Trial (1945)

The Indian National Army trials (also known as the INA trials and the Red Fort trials) was the British Indian trial by court-martial of a number of officers of the Indian National Army (INA) between November 1945 and May 1946, on various charges of treason, torture, murder and abetment to murder, during the Second World War. The accused had a large number of other troops and officers of the British Indian Army, joined the Indian National Army and later fought in Burma alongside the Japanese military under the Azad Hind.

The Indian Independence League, a civilian political body, was formed to oversee the army between March and June 1942. Rashbehari Bose, a revolutionary who had taken refuge in Japan, was elected president of the League. A formal decision to raise the INA was taken, with Captain Mohan Singh as its commander. By the end of 1942, the INA's strength reached 40,000 soldiers. In 1943, Subhas Chandra Bose, who had escaped from India in 1941, was invited to lead the INA. Bose established the Provisional Government of Free India, recognized by eight nations, including Germany and Italy, and assumed the role of Supreme Commander of the INA. The INA was organized into three brigades: Gandhi Brigade, Azad Brigade, and Nehru Brigade.

A women's regiment, the Rani Jhansi Brigade, commanded by Captain Lakshmi Sehgal, was also established, symbolising a revolutionary step in women's involvement in armed struggle.

In 1944, INA regiments marched alongside the Japanese army to enter India through Burma, with a plan to capture Imphal and advance into Assam.

The INA marked a pivotal moment in the participation of women in India's national movement. Fifteen hundred women from various socio-economic backgrounds volunteered for the Rani Jhansi Brigade.

Though initially assigned non-combat roles, they earned recognition as combatants during the Imphal campaign of 1945. This involvement significantly transitioned from passive resistance to heroic activism, setting a precedent for women's role in future movements.

The INA demonstrated remarkable communal harmony among Hindu, Muslim, and Sikh soldiers, fighting as Indians rather than representatives of specific religions. The Rani Jhansi Brigade symbolized a shift in women's roles, showing their potential as combatants in the national struggle. The INA received immense contributions from expatriate Indians, highlighting their dedication to India's freedom. The INA's campaign shattered the British illusion of Indian soldiers' unwavering loyalty, undermining a key pillar of their imperial rule.

The INA's efforts, despite their military failure, left a lasting legacy. They challenged British colonial authority, inspired mass agitations, and united Indians across diverse backgrounds. The INA trials and subsequent public upheavals played a crucial role in weakening British resolve, contributing significantly to the final push for India's independence.

Chapter 69:

Barelvi Movement

The Barelvi movement is a remarkable Islamic religious movement within Sunni Islam. It takes its name from the town of Bareilly in northern India, where it originated in the 19th century. The followers of this movement are known as Barelvis.

The Barelvi movement emerged as a response to the spread of the Deobandi movement, another prominent Sunni Islamic movement in South Asia. The followers of the Deobandi movement advocated for a strict and conservative interpretation of Islam, promoting the purging of what they considered innovations (Bida'h) in religious practices. The Barelvis also maintain a strong tradition of visiting and seeking blessings from the graves of Sufi saints and promoting Sufi practices. Religious reform movements like the Barelvi Movement played a key role in shaping modern Indian society by fostering religious and cultural continuity among followers. The Barelvi Movement, under Ahmed Raza Khan, emphasized devotion to the Prophet Muhammad, veneration of saints, and adherence to traditional Sunni practices in the face of reformist challenges. It provided a unifying platform for many Indian Muslims, strengthening their religious identity and resisting puritanical influences. By advocating for the preservation of Sufi traditions and spiritual practices, the movement influenced socio-religious dynamics and contributed to the diversity of India's Islamic landscape, shaping the cultural and communal identity of its adherents.

Maulvi Syed Ahmad Rai Barelvi is regarded as a 'Shaheed' (Islamic martyr) by nearly all Deobandi and Ahle Hadisi adherents because he was killed while waging militant jihad against non-Muslims in undivided India. The increased historical and ideological implications of Syed Ahmad Rai Barelvi's Mujahidin movement piqued the interest of classical Islamic scholars.

BARELVI MOVEMENT

Chapter 70:

Madurai Conspiracy Case (1945)

The Madurai Conspiracy Case, also known as the Madurai Bomb Case, was a vital legal and political event that took place in India during the pre-independence era. It occurred in 1945, during British colonial rule in the country. The case involved a conspiracy to overthrow British rule through violent means.

A & F Harvey mills was the biggest mill in Tamil Nadu. Its unit in Madurai had about twelve thousand workers and Ambasamudram and Tuticorin units, about six thousand workers. Madurai Labour Union (MLU) was the only union in the mill which was led by S.R.V. Naidu, a confidant of Harvey mills management. An anti-Communist by nature, he refused to enrol Communist workers in his union. In 1943, Naidu made an agreement with the management to keep the bonus of the workers in the savings fund. Workers protested against this agreement and 7 Communists who led this struggle were arrested and sent to jail for six months. Left with no other alternative, Ramamurti decided to start the All India Trade Union and it started functioning from the month of October with Ramamurti as its president. In 1946, Harvey mill management dismissed 27 workers stating that they worked against the recognised union. The union started a strong resistance movement against the dismissals. The Government referred the matter to arbitration. Ramamurti himself represented the union and argued against the dismissal. During the course of this argument, he demanded a secret ballot to determine the representative character of the union and said if his union did not get the majority, he would dissolve his union. Finally the arbitrator ordered the reinstatement of 27 workers, and also to hold elections through secret ballot to find out the representative character of the union. In the elections Communist union won with a thumping majority and got recognition. This victory became a morale booster for the Communist Party in Madurai district and its influence began to spread to other areas. The British Government wanted to curb the Communist movement in Madurai. They arrested Ramamurti, N. Sankaraiah, K. T. K. Thangamani and many others started the Madurai Conspiracy case. The main charge was that Ramamurti and other leaders were hatching a conspiracy at the party office to physically eliminate other trade union leaders; this was overheard by a cart puller who reported it to the police. Ramamurti and others were released from jail and thousands of workers with red flags who waited outside the jail gate took them in procession. Ramamurti and other leaders addressed a vast gathering.

The Madurai Conspiracy Case played a crucial role in galvanizing the Indian independence movement and further strengthened the resolve of the Indian people to achieve freedom from British rule. It also brought attention to the use of repressive measures by the colonial authorities to suppress dissent and nationalist activities in the country.

MADURAI CONSPIRANCY CASE (1945)

Chapter 71:

RIN Mutiny (1946)

The Royal Indian Navy (RIN) Mutiny of 1946 was a significant event in India's struggle for independence from British colonial rule. The mutiny occurred among Indian sailors in the Royal Indian Navy, which was composed of Indian personnel serving under British officers.

The RIN Mutiny was triggered by several factors, including low pay, harsh working conditions, and a lack of opportunities for Indian sailors to rise to higher ranks. Additionally, there was a growing sense of discontent and a desire for independence among the Indian military personnel.

The immediate cause of the mutiny was the ill-treatment of a ratings (enlisted sailors) delegation that went to meet with senior naval officers to discuss their grievances. The delegation was arrested, which further inflamed tensions.

Chapter 72:

Cabinet Mission Plan (1946)

The Cabinet Mission Plan was a momentous initiative undertaken by the British government in 1946 to address the political deadlock and communal tensions in India during its struggle for independence. The plan was formulated by a three-member delegation, known as the Cabinet Mission, which was sent to India in March 1946.

The Cabinet Mission consisted of the following members:

- Lord Pethick-Lawrence: Secretary of State for India

- Sir Stafford Cripps: President of the Board of Trade

- A.V. Alexander: First Lord of the Admiralty

The primary objective of the Cabinet Mission was to propose a framework for the establishment of a united and independent India. The Cabinet Mission was a great plan that aimed to make a Constituent Assembly of India and avoid the partition..

CABINET MISSION PLAN (1946)

Chapter 73:

Harsha Chhina Mogha Morcha (1946–47)

Harse Chhina Mogha Morcha was an agrarian revolt in Punjab that took place in 1946– 1947. The campaign was launched in June 1946 by remodelling the moghas (canal outlets) under the leadership of the Communist Party, which was later joined by all major political parties of the time, to stand against the decision of the British Government to decrease the supply of irrigation water to farmers. The campaign was headed by Comrade Achhar Singh Chhina, Sohan Singh Josh, Mohan Singh Batth, Baba Karam Singh Cheema, Jagbir Singh Chhina, and Gurdial Singh Dhillon, etc. During the campaign all prominent leaders along with more than a thousand remonstrating peasants were arrested by the police and detained in Lahore Jail for three months. As a result of this movement, the British Government agreed to provide more farming water to agriculturists as per the previous agreed terms.

Chapter 74:

Tebhaga Movement (1946–1947)

Tebhaga movement (1946–1947) was symbolic peasant agitation, initiated in Bengal by the All India Kisan Sabha of the peasant front, of the Communist Party of India.

It was an intense peasant movement in the history of India. It was a fierce peasant uprising on the eve of India's independence and the partition of Bengal. The Tebhaga movement also laid the groundwork for future land reform movements in India. After India gained independence in 1947, land reform measures were introduced to address the issues faced by the rural population, and several states enacted laws to protect tenant farmers' rights and provide them with more equitable conditions. The movement's emphasis on the rights of the peasants and its association with leftist ideologies also contributed to the development of agrarian politics and the broader peasant movements in India.

The movement brought the issue of land reforms to the forefront of the political agenda in Bengal. Although the immediate demands of the movement were not met, it laid the groundwork for future land reforms, including the abolition of the zamindari system and the redistribution of land. The movement contributed to a heightened political consciousness among the peasantry in Bengal. It demonstrated the potential of organised peasant resistance and the need for political representation of agrarian interests. The Tebhaga Movement was part of the broader wave of agrarian struggles that swept across India in the 1940s. These movements played a crucial role in challenging the legitimacy of colonial rule and contributed to the momentum for India's independence. Women played a significant role in the movement, forming groups like the 'Nari Bahini' to defend the rights of sharecroppers, which broadened the base of the women's movement in India. The Tebhaga Movement impacted subsequent agrarian movements in India, including the Telangana

Rebellion and the Naxalite movement. It remains a symbol of peasant resistance against economic exploitation and injustice.

The Tebhaga movement is probably the greatest peasant movement in the history of India.

TEBHAGA MOVEMENT (1946 – 1947)

Chapter 75:

India Independence Act (1947)

The Indian Independence Act (1947) marked the formal end of British rule in India. It provided for the partition of India into two separate countries, India and Pakistan, and granted them independence. The Act also established the principles for the division of assets and delineation of boundaries. It declared India as an independent and sovereign state.

The Act declared India as a sovereign and independent state. It also made provisions for the partition of the Indian state into two separate dominions of India and Pakistan on grounds of religious differences. The position of the Secretary of States for India was abolished.The office of the Viceroy was also abolished and the Act initiated for the providence of two separate Governor-Generals to be appointed for the dominions of India and Pakistan on the advice of the British Cabinet. The Constituent Assemblies of both the dominions were authorised to formulate their respective constitutions and also to repeal any law of the British Parliament formulated for the Indian state, including the Independence Act itself. The Constituent Assemblies were empowered to act as legislative bodies for their respective dominions till the time they could formulate a constitution for their state. It granted authority to the princely states to join either of the dominions or remain independent. The governance of each dominion was to be done on the basis of the Government of India Act, of 1935. The British Monarch no longer had the authority to veto or ask for the bills of the Indian state. The Governor-General of each dominion had to act on the advice of the council. The Radcliffe Commission was immediately appointed following the Act to draw up boundaries between the two dominions. The borders were drawn based on religious differences. The states of Punjab and Bengal were divided between the two dominions.

Lord Louis Mountbatten became the Governor-General of India, while Muhammad Ali Jinnah became the Governor-General of Pakistan.

Pandit Jawaharlal Nehru became the prime minister of India, while Liaqat Ali Khan became his Pakistani counterpart.

The Indian Independence Act paved the way for the independence of the states of India and Pakistan. The British Crown completely transferred the power to the newly formed states. The suzerainty of the British was abolished. However, it was accompanied by the violent partition, which remains one of the largest forced migrations in the history of the world, in which millions perished.

INDIA INDEPENDENCE ACT (1947)

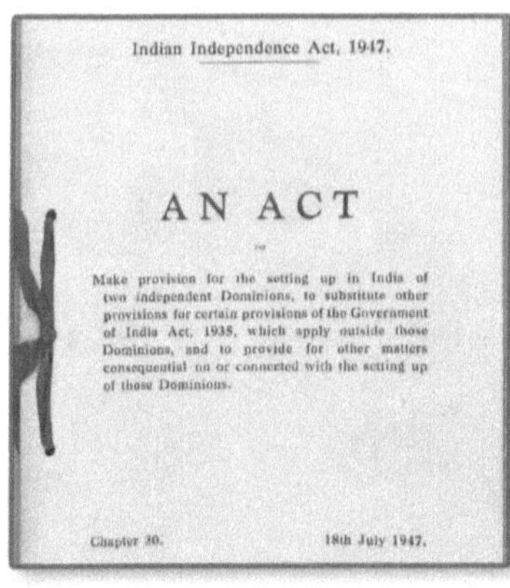

"Author's Purpose"

The decision to publish a book on 75 freedom movements in India stems from the desire to celebrate and honor the immense sacrifices, resilience, and collective efforts that shaped India's journey to independence. Here are the key reasons behind this endeavor:

1. Commemorating 75 Years of Independence

As India celebrates 75 years of independence, it is the perfect occasion to reflect on and pay tribute to the significant milestones in its freedom struggle. The number "75" symbolizes a significant milestone in India's history, as the country celebrated its 75th anniversary of independence recently. This book serves as a tribute to the countless known and unknown heroes who contributed to the nation's liberation.

2. Highlighting Diversity in the Freedom Struggle

By documenting 75 movements, the book showcases the multifaceted nature of India's struggle and emphasizes the inclusivity of the independence movement.

3. Bringing Lesser-Known Struggles to Light

While major movements like the Non-Cooperation Movement and Quit India Movement are widely recognized, numerous local and grassroots revolts, tribal uprisings, and reformist efforts remain underrepresented in mainstream narratives. This book aims to highlight many such lesser-known yet crucial contributions to India's independence.

4. Educating and Inspiring Future Generations

The book serves as a resource to educate readers, especially the younger generation, about the sacrifices and ideals that led to India's freedom. It aims to instill a sense of pride, patriotism, and a deeper understanding of the values of justice, unity, and equality. By compiling these movements, the author may have hoped to create an accessible, enduring resource for future citizens to reconnect with their history and gain pride from it.

5. Rediscovering India's Hidden Heroes

With time, the stories of many movements risk being forgotten. This book seeks to preserve these accounts as a historical legacy, ensuring that the contributions of all regions, communities, and leaders are remembered and celebrated.

6. Promoting Unity and National Pride

By chronicling the collective efforts of Indians from all walks of life, the book reinforces the spirit of unity and the shared aspiration for freedom. It serves as a reminder of what India can achieve when united by a common cause. By showcasing movements from all corners of the country, I want to promote a sense of national unity, reminding readers that despite differences, the country stood together for independence.

7. A Tribute to the Spirit of Freedom

Each movement highlighted in the book represents the indomitable spirit of resistance, courage, and hope that defined India's fight against colonial oppression. Publishing this book is a way of honoring that spirit and keeping it alive for generations to come.

In essence, this book is not just a collection of events; it is a celebration of India's resilience, a homage to its heroes, and a source of inspiration for the future.

"To our beloved freedom fighters,

You fought with courage we can hardly fathom. Today, we live the dream you envisioned. This book is my humble tribute to your sacrifices, a reminder to the generations yet to come to never take freedom for granted. Beyond the renowned leaders, countless unsung heroes fought in quiet but powerful ways for freedom. Your stories remind us that change often begins in small, selfless acts of courage."

Message for the Present and Future Generation

Writing this book was a journey into the heart of a time that transformed the world. My hope is that readers will see its echoes in our lives today and be inspired to learn more. Freedom is not just a gift from the past but a responsibility for the future. The rights we enjoy today were hard-won, reminding us that liberty must be guarded, nurtured, and cherished.

In a country as diverse as ours, the freedom movement proved that unity is our greatest strength. The movement for freedom planted a vast banyan tree—its roots deep, its branches sheltering. But like any tree, it requires care and nurturing to ensure it grows stronger for generations to come. As we face modern challenges, this unity must be the foundation of our progress.

Let us carry forward the lessons of the past as we strive to create a future worthy of the sacrifices made by those who came before us. The legacy of these events continues to shape our present, serving as a reminder of the resilience and potential of humanity in the face of adversity.

"The flames of the freedom movement have illuminated a path for future generations. It is now their turn to walk this road and forge a brighter tomorrow. It was not one language, one religion, or one region that brought freedom, but the harmonious symphony of many. This unity in diversity remains India's greatest triumph and responsibility."

In 2022, Dr Mili received the "***Outstanding Women Award***" for raising awareness of Indian culture abroad from *Women Icon powered by Times Women.*

In 2024, Dr Mili was honored with the "***Global Indian Cultural Icon Award***" by Indian Police Mitra Bharat & Dr. DS Rathod & Marshal Yoga Academy,